You

ransformation

AISHA ALIM

Dedication

To all those individuals who have ever had their confidence shattered and are wanting to rebuild it – this book is for you.

Disclaimer:

The material in this publication is of the nature of general advice only and does not replace professional advice. It is not a substitute for other professional services such as counselling or therapy and does not diagnose or treat any disorders nor is it a replacement of such. The material contained in this publication is not a substitute for other professional services such as legal, medical or business issues and the reader is therefore responsible for their own decisions and wellbeing. Readers are responsible for the actions they take and as such, the author is not legally responsible for any and all outside parties' wellbeing, thoughts, feelings, actions and decisions they make and therefore, is not liable for the resultant outcomes. To the maximum extent permitted by law, the author and publisher and all associated parties and affiliates, disclaim all responsibility and liability, to any person arising directly or indirectly from the actions individuals take based on the information contained within this publication.

It's All Within You

Tools for Transformation

AISHA ALIM

ISBN: 978-0-646-82789-6

A CIP catalogue record for this book is available from the British Library.

Edited by Aisha Alim

Cover Design and Typesetting: Jen Parker, Fuzzy Flamingo
www.fuzzyflamingo.co.uk

Dedication

To all those individuals who have ever had their confidence shattered and are wanting to rebuild it – this book is for you.

Disclaimer:

The material in this publication is of the nature of general advice only and does not replace professional advice. It is not a substitute for other professional services such as counselling or therapy and does not diagnose or treat any disorders nor is it a replacement of such. The material contained in this publication is not a substitute for other professional services such as legal, medical or business issues and the reader is therefore responsible for their own decisions and wellbeing. Readers are responsible for the actions they take and as such, the author is not legally responsible for any and all outside parties' wellbeing, thoughts, feelings, actions and decisions they make and therefore, is not liable for the resultant outcomes. To the maximum extent permitted by law, the author and publisher and all associated parties and affiliates, disclaim all responsibility and liability, to any person arising directly or indirectly from the actions individuals take based on the information contained within this publication.

Praise for It's All Within You

"*It's All Within You* is a type of book, which as you navigate through it, you cannot help but sense that it is reading you. It's filled with wisdom and guidance to help you transform into the best version of you that you can. Each chapter seems like a stand-alone tale about your inner self-talk, making it reader-friendly, so you can start anywhere you want and navigate through it in any order you choose. Under each topic, it dives into your psychological and emotional patterns of thinking, extracts, pinpoints and articulates your self-talk and where they're coming from.

The author, Aisha, skilfully translates your conscious and subconscious thoughts into strikingly relatable phrases and sentences that make you admit to yourself, 'that's exactly what I say and do to myself'. But she then inspires and guides you on how to manoeuvre and manage yourself out of it in a simple, practical and realistic way. She knows what she is talking about.

After reading it, you'll discover that you start to automatically 'catch' yourself when negative beliefs, thoughts and habits get to you and how to counsel yourself, by yourself, in your day to day life.

This is a book which teaches emotional intelligence on a deeper level; a valuable knowledge and skill so direly needed in today's society to thrive and peacefully reach success."

Belal Assaad
International motivational speaker

"*It's All Within You* allows for deep self-reflection to transform your life, providing practical tools to assist, guide and inspire transformation. You have the choice to change."

Heather Urie
English Channel team relay swimmer 2019

"Aisha has crafted into one body of work, what every person struggling needs to read. The topics discussed within are what holds people back from greatness and Aisha shows you how to break free."

Sean Douglas
TEDx Speaker, Business Positioning strategist, International radio show host, International bestselling author

"Aisha is living her passion through her inspiration and wisdom in a quest to inspire many others to live their best life ever moving forward. When you read, *It's All Within You*, you find it's not just another personal development or self-help book, it's a hands on guide that will empower you through her experiences and knowledge.

As an entrepreneur, who has read many personal development books, this book moved me with its practical and personal insights. It will guide you to being the 'best' possible you!

I recommend obtaining a copy of this book to add to your must read list."

Lourene Bevaart
5 x World Karate champion
Australian team captain
TV Gladiator's series two winner
Gladiator – Glacier
Personal trainer to Russell Crowe and Shane Warne
Entrepreneur

About the author

Aisha is an empowerment coach, speaker, consultant, mentor, facilitator and now a published author. She is a mother and a former primary school teacher with a Diploma and Bachelor's degree. She has undergone training in life coaching including Meta Dynamics and NLP and brings a wealth of knowledge and experience in running workshops. Aisha has successfully completed her Mental Health First Aid training and recently undertook a body language course with world renowned experts, Greg Hartley and Scott Rouse to further her expertise. She has presented topics she is particularly passionate about as a public speaker in a variety of settings over many years.

In 2017 she turned her attention specifically to life coaching and facilitating adult workshops, with a passion in helping people find their purpose, overcome fear and developing confidence. She takes a very balanced view of things and believes true authenticity comes from experience and a willingness to learn.

Aisha has worked in many industries in a variety of roles including management and training others in leadership development. She has always been highly sought after for her wisdom and advice from a very young age and has a proven track record in helping clients live authentic, happy lives. She is actively coaching multiple clients, running self-empowerment courses and a range of professional development workshops. With over twenty-five years' experience, she aims to take her workshops worldwide to audiences seeking to better themselves and welcomes the opportunity to do so. She continues to be involved in her local community with a particular interest in teaching dance and umpiring hockey. She also serves on a local committee.

Aisha has a firm and fair approach and is warm and engaging. She is vivacious by nature and always aims to deliver value. She hopes every person walks away feeling empowered and ready to change their lives by implementing these tried and tested tools.

Contents

Introduction

When I first thought about writing a book the very idea terrified me. The what if's started to rear their heads and I began to question whether or not I was capable of doing it. What if I fail, what if it isn't any good, what if no-one likes it, what if, what if, what if? These rhetorical questions that serve only to disempower, were sneaking their way back in and the irony was, I was allowing them to. These useless sentiments that seem to be our constant companion whenever we try something new had to be stopped. The only way that was going to happen, was by putting these words down on paper, by taking action and having a go.

To do nothing is action as well; it's comfortable to stagnate, it doesn't challenge a person to reach their full potential and more often than not, that frightens people to death. I knew within the very core of my being that I could do it, but to procrastinate and find excuses why I couldn't do this was far easier, or so I told myself. The fact was, I was choosing not to do it and that was a bitter pill to swallow at first.

I'd previously had a go at writing some smaller books none of which made it further than being printed and bound and certainly not in the hands of a publisher. They were good confidence builders and a great practice run for this book, but this time I felt a renewed vigour and a deeper sense of confidence to have a go and do it. How else was I going to know if I could do it, unless I had a go and allowed others to read it and assess it for themselves? I wouldn't.

As a former school teacher, I know I can sometimes get caught up in the semantics of whether everything is right or not, instead of allowing myself the freedom to just do it. There are spell checkers and editors to check over things, so why was I finding excuses not to write? I knew why I felt that way, it was because I feared failing and it was easier to stay comfortable where I was. It was easier to find a reason *not* to do it, to allow excuses to pile up and justify why I couldn't put pen to paper. I recognised the blocks I was beginning to put up by building that wall of fear again. I was allowing the fear of being rejected and not being good enough to take over instead of freeing myself and doing it. Brick by brick that wall had to be broken. It had to come down.

The only way to achieve true personal success is to do the things we fear the most. It would only be overcome by having a go, taking that leap of faith and being courageous enough to push outside my comfort zone and do it. It's only then that true growth of self happens.

So here it is. My first book. My first *real* go of writing something that is of value to others, based not only on what I've learned, but from personal experience as well. I've done the hard yards by letting go of the past and only looking forward and this is the result.

My aim throughout the book is to give you a mixture of information, tools, strategies and some exercises for you to do as well. I have also used examples from clients (by their permission of course), so it is easier for you to relate to. I would encourage you to participate along with me as you read to help you get the most from this book. You'll notice as you read through the book there are certain aspects I repeat in other chapters. I've done this for two reasons; to reinforce what you learn and secondly, these tools are not stand alone and separate from one another – they cross over.

Primarily, the aim of doing this book is to give you as much information as I can to help you live a more authentic and happier life, to help you tap back into those inner qualities and build your self-confidence. With each step you take with me, by reading the pages and doing the suggested activities, my sincere hope is you walk away from reading this feeling empowered and invigorated.

So sit back and get ready to embrace new understandings to apply in your life of these tried and tested methods I share in this book. Be prepared to be as authentic and as honest with yourself as possible. The journey isn't easy at times, but it is one that is worth the ride. I truly hope that you end up living your ultimate life by becoming a better you – the best you yet. The one you were born to be.

To do nothing is to do something and to do nothing won't change your life. Only you have the power to do so. It's all within you.

A PURPOSEFUL LIFE

Life is full of many tests
Of which we hope to pass,
Along the way lessons learned,
From experiences from our past.

The road is full of twists and turns,
At times it's hard to see,
Through murky waters trying to find,
That better version of me.

'Coz ultimately it seems to be,
A goal one does desire,
To be thoughtful, loving, caring and kind,
Remembered and admired.

That destiny of finding purpose
Of having a heart content,
Forgiveness, courage, doing hard yards,
And moments to self-reflect.

When all aligned and values in-tact,
That self-belief does rise,
It overflows; it wants to give back,
And allow others to arrive.

Newcomers come a-knocking,
Wanting the same as they see,
How do I become just like that?
A better version of me?

And so the cycle continues,
To find purpose and meaning in life,
It dares to become the greatest challenge,
We all do recognise.

It takes patience, persistence and lifelong learning,
To refine, reflect and repeat,
As the ultimate state of perfection is,
A purposeful life well lived.

Knowledge is Power
Power is Strength
Strength is Courage
Courage is Discipline
Discipline is Order
Order is Change
Change is Good
Good is Love
Love is Respect
Respect is Man
Man is Made
Made by Who?
Made by God.

Tool 1

∽═╾

Understanding where it all starts

"Values are the deeply held beliefs that drive and direct your behaviour."

Glenn C Stewart

Every human being regardless of where they're born, who their parents are, or where they grew up, have a view (or map) of the world, that has been formed primarily as a result of the surroundings they've been in and are currently in right now. No two people look at things in the same way as one another. Two people could be standing together seeing a view of mountains with a backdrop of blue sky, but how each of them interprets what they see transpires into their map of the world.

If asked what they see, one could go into a lot of detail about the formation of the mountains, how they're expansive, set apart from the greenery of the trees that sit at the foot of the mountain and the sky is a piercing blue. The other could describe things very differently; describing the snow-capped mountains and only the etchings of dark images of birds piercing the skyline.

Two people seeing the same image; the sky, the mountains and the trees – they're the facts that are unchangeable. However, what we see here is that each one is interpreting what they see based on their paradigms (or maps of the world) and communicating two very different viewpoints. It doesn't mean one is right and the other is wrong, it just means that each person sees things differently and we need to respect that. We need to be mindful that just because we see things a certain way, doesn't mean that others have to see them that way too. We have to learn to understand that their map is their map just like ours is ours.

Sometimes unnecessary arguments or misunderstandings happen, as a result of our expectations that others *should* see things how we do and 'why can't they see it from my point of view' are the type of statements that follow. The point is, we all view the world very differently, even though the world is the world the facts of it don't change, it's how we interact with one another and the world in which we live that are different. Many things affect our map and it's ever-changing as we grow and learn in life, but if we aren't willing to be honest with ourselves, to want more for ourselves and understand we are worthy of more, it will never come to be. The only way to get the most from life is to expect the most from ourselves first.

But how are paradigms formed in the first place and what influences them? Each of our maps of the world are going to be different from the other, but primarily, the map is highly influenced and formed by family – in the environment in which we grew up in. The family's values, attitudes and beliefs are the foundations that form how we feel about ourselves and how we interact and deal with other people. They're the foundational building blocks that over time grow and form each of our set of core principles and form the basis of how we respond to different situations. As Stephen Covey stated in his book titled, *The Seven Habits of Highly Effective People*, "We see the world, not as *it is*, but as *we are* – or, as we are conditioned to see it. When we open our mouths to describe what we see, we in effect describe ourselves, our perceptions, our paradigms."

The problem is that when someone disagrees with us about what we see, such as the mountains and sky example, we automatically think there is something wrong with *them*. Why can't they see what I'm seeing? What do you mean when you say that? That's not right, this is. It's the 'I'm right and you're wrong' mentality. These types of statements are usually what occurs when two people cannot see things from another's perspective and disagreements can occur when an individual's map collides with another's and no common or middle ground is achieved. Both parties walk away feeling frustrated, rejected or misunderstood, when the problem could quite easily have been solved by a genuine interest in seeking to understand the other person's viewpoint and not seeking to validate and defend their own map.

The family unit we are born into, the unit that raises us from small children (in whatever format of a family that is), builds and forms the basis of our character. It's here that the foundations are set, values and beliefs are instilled and how we respond to things is determined. It can be one of two broad environments on a very long spectrum to be immersed in. On one end is a healthy and functional and deeply resourceful unit and the second unhealthy, dysfunctional and unresourceful.

The continuum from healthy and resourceful to unhealthy and unresourceful is full of many variables. No one family unit is perfect in every sense of the word and no one family is completely dysfunctional either. Each family is governed by its own set of principles, its own set of rules, responsibilities and expectations for each member. It's here that beliefs about ourselves and the world around us and what we value in life are shaped and formed. How we're raised in this environment more often than not, determines our level of self-worth and confidence levels, which affects how we interact with others and how functional we become in society as well.

Our view of the world on the surface is shaped by our thoughts, attitudes and behaviours. Think of them like healthy green foliage on a tree. To examine our paradigms to be effective, resourceful, functioning human beings, we need to go deeper. We need to look further than the foliage and examine the trunk itself. We need to look at our maps and how they were formed and examine our core being. Without this deeper exploration, without a sincere and honest examination of how our attitudes, feelings and behaviours were shaped in the first place, the task is fruitless. In other words, without a good hard look at our inner core selves, nothing we change will be long-lasting – it will only be superficial. It will only address the foliage issue and not the tree itself.

If our maps we have created are not in line with our values and beliefs then problems will arise. If we are living a life that is not congruent with being honest and trustworthy for example, then feelings of confusion and conflict will rise to the surface. This is due to outward actions colliding with the natural instincts to be trustworthy and honest, leading to a feeling of inner conflict. If this path is followed, we will be lead down a road of dysfunction and loss and issues such as anti-social behaviour, outbursts of anger and frustration will occur. However, if we recognise these internal conflicts and want the very best life has to offer us, we must first examine ourselves and our paradigms, to get to the heart of the matter – the trunk of the tree and not just the foliage. The road of self-discovery and wanting more from life can be long and arduous at times, but one worth taking to live happily and to become functioning, contributing members of society as well.

If the map of the world that has been imparted to us does not align with our primary beliefs and values, then the map itself needs a deeper examination. It needs to be examined to see if the map is distorted and whether further outside assistance would be beneficial in changing it. Just like the tree, it often takes us until adulthood when our roots are established, when we are older and wiser, to develop a desire to understand ourselves more. We seek clarity on issues and answers to questions we may have had lingering in the background for many years, wondering why a sense of confusion was always with us. Many of these thoughts could be summarised into 'it must be me, there's something wrong with me' type sentiments, as we often blame ourselves first before looking elsewhere.

This is particularly true for people who have experienced some type of trauma during childhood where their trust has been broken. People who have experienced violence in the home for example, often grow up with trust issues, because they've had their trust broken over and over and sometimes for years on end. It becomes normal, expected even, that people will inevitably let you down, that the only person you can rely on is yourself and men aren't to be trusted. In this instance, the issue about trusting people has carried forward into adulthood. There is the internal conflict that trust should be a given, that it should be expected that your family members can be trusted with anything and everything, yet in the case of growing up in a household of domestic violence, that trust was continually broken. Not only that, in the most vulnerable state as children, when trust is broken, it is a natural reaction to not want to expose that vulnerability again, to avoid getting hurt in an attempt to protect ourselves. This is all completely normal.

However, that reaction has now caused issues around trusting men and can subconsciously motivate us to self-sabotage a perfectly good relationship so we don't get hurt. We fear being vulnerable, fear exposing the very core of ourselves, because the fear of that happening just one more time is too much pain to bear and believe it's better to shut down. Alternatively, another way of protecting self is deliberately provoking an argument. 'I knew he would leave' is a common sentiment of women raised in these type of environments and tend to see how far they can push, so they can validate themselves and say 'I was right'. It's a vicious cycle they create for themselves; wanting love, but too frightened to be vulnerable again in case they get hurt. It's a way of protecting by provoking, as they haven't yet learned how real love works. When enough is enough and he decides to leave, they've reinforced a negative image of themselves by sabotaging the relationship and once again, feel unworthy of love.

This cycle of negative outcomes for relationships can be due to the lack of positive male role models growing up and not observing mature, loving and caring interactions between parents. Not knowing how couples can be equally supporting one another throughout life, they cling to a fear based map in an attempt to find the boundaries of his love and acceptance. They haven't learned how to have that genuineness in a relationship for themselves and by the time they do learn, it's usually too late.

That deep seeded fear that resulted out of that child's trust being abused and broken for so many years, has left the adult version of themselves in tatters with their core values. This is a prime example of inner conflict, of questions about why their relationships keep failing and the men in their lives keep leaving them. The 'it must be my fault' validation in stark contrast to the core value of trust in its purest form. This person's map as a result of one core value in turmoil, has resulted in a sweeping generalisation about themselves and the world around them. In this case, 'that all men can't be trusted, they'll only hurt me and leave me, what's the point of having a relationship in the first place if this is what will happen each time and it's all my fault'. If this map (or view of things) was carried throughout their entire lives, imagine the possibilities they would deprive themselves of. Imagine not experiencing the joy of a beautiful, healthy relationship on every level with that special someone of the opposite sex.

Quite possibly so many wonderful opportunities gone begging and missed out on, because they allowed the fear of rejection, the fear of not being good enough to take over. They weren't courageous enough to take that leap of faith and give it a go, to prove their generalisations about men wrong and learn new skills to stop sabotaging their relationships. They gave into fear. Moreover, they did the greatest disservice to themselves because they were not willing to examine their own map of the world. To examine their beliefs and values and see if they were in line with who they truly are inside – the trunk and not just the leaves. What a tragedy it would be if they had chosen not to self-examine and learn new skills to empower themselves, to live a life that's worth so much more than what they're currently settling for.

We all need to continually self-assess to check in with our core values and beliefs and see if they are in line with our view of the world and our unique purpose. It can be as simple as doing a journal or as intensive as you decide it to be. Each person is different, every person's map of the world is to be respected, but my hope is that every person continually improves themselves to ultimately live a very fulfilling and happier life.

Beliefs

Every person has a set of beliefs that help define and shape their lives. Our beliefs are primarily formed by the experiences we have and by the people we surround ourselves with. They affect the way we think about ourselves, others and the world around us and they greatly influence our emotions and our actions. According to the Oxford dictionary, a belief is defined as *an opinion about something; something that you think is true.* Our beliefs are developed as a result of being passed down to us first through our families and secondly, they're influenced by our circle of friends. They are also highly influenced throughout our lives based on the experiences we encounter. Our reality of how we interact with the world is made up of what we believe. We subconsciously look for evidence to prove or disprove a belief we hold, which then determines what actions we take.

When I was very sick for many years one of the beliefs I held was, 'I'll never have my health'. This belief didn't help me and for many years I looked for evidence to prove this to be true. It was affirmed for a long time by the health professionals caring for me, but when I decided to self-evaluate and reflect, I realised that this belief was holding me back. The reality was that I was ill. However, the belief I had firmly fixed in my mind had to be changed. What made this even harder was that concerned family members and others around me were affirming this belief as true and that my circumstances were unlikely to change. On top of that, I was being validated with sympathy – that I had a genuine reason for feeling sorry for myself because of my illness at the time. I felt stuck. The problem was it became a self-perpetuating cycle that left me with little or no hope that things could ever be different. Not the way I had envisioned my life to be. If things didn't change, I would continue throughout my life believing the fact that my health would never improve and, therefore, I would not live up to my full potential as a human being. I'd continue to limit myself based on this belief which determined the actions (or lack thereof), I would take to improve things for myself.

When we are born we are like a blank slate waiting to be filled in with information via all our senses. Our parents, siblings and significant others play a huge role in imparting beliefs to us as children and being impressionable, we automatically look for meaning in almost everything we do because we are naturally inquisitive. We are also greatly influenced by what experiences we have. Sometimes these experiences aren't pleasant and as such they leave their mark.

For example, let's say growing up that at times you didn't finish your dinner because you weren't feeling hungry and were scolded by your parents for not eating all of your food. They may have told you that there are starving children around the world who aren't as fortunate as you are and who would be grateful to have what you're having. It may be said (or implied), that by not finishing you were being ungrateful. If you took what your parents said to be true and more often than not we do, then this has planted a seed of belief around not finishing your meals. By association, the belief that only good boys and girls eat all their food up, that you're not a good person if you don't, has also been sewn into your subconscious. On top of that, you're also being ungrateful and selfish, because children who are starving could have eaten it and now the belief of being selfish has been planted as well. Each time you don't finish and are chastised about it, the more those beliefs get cemented.

Another example of a belief we take for granted as being true is the existence of Santa Claus or the Easter Bunny. I certainly remember believing them to be real and again, the associated behaviour of being good to receive any presents or gifts was reinforced many times. If I misbehaved around Christmas time, the fear of not being good enough to receive a present from Santa was firmly ingrained in my mind. That's how impressionable we are as children; we are that blank slate waiting to be filled in with beliefs that serve us or beliefs that don't. In the above examples, those beliefs I had as a child certainly didn't serve me in later years.

When we get older we are also greatly influenced by our teachers and classmates. Let's assume you are bullied by other kids who continually tell you that you are fat, ugly or uncool. After a while, you might start believing this to be fact and start perceiving yourself as fat, ugly and uncool because of the consistency of what's being said to you. They may even get physically abusive towards you and consequently you may believe that you are weak because of your inability to defend yourself.

When we accept something to be fact and form a belief, it is stored in our subconscious mind. Our subconscious mind does not know (or care for that matter), if the belief is true or false. It stores it as fact for later use to make things easier by automating our actions and responses to certain situations. When crossing the street, you know to look both ways because you have been taught that and have held onto that belief. This is a good example of a belief that has been stored that serves us in a positive and helpful way.

Once formed, beliefs become ingrained in our subconscious and act as a guide through life. We don't think about them we just take them for granted that they are there. It's when a person decides to take a closer look at themselves and realise they're worth more, that a closer examination of their beliefs is a worthwhile activity to do. Our beliefs determine if we consider something or someone to be good or bad, right or wrong, nice or nasty, safe or dangerous, acceptable or unacceptable and so on. Our beliefs about ourselves also dictate what is possible or achievable and this can be limiting or limitless. Depending on which one it is, that will equate to the outcome.

If I had continued to believe that writing a book was only for people who were famous and who were good at it, I'd never be sitting here writing these words. If I'd held onto that limiting belief, then I wouldn't have achieved the goal of publishing this book. It was through self-reflecting and challenging those beliefs I had about myself and believing I could do it, that I was able to change that belief and achieve my goal. That became a limitless belief and the old belief was replaced by a positive and achievable one.

A good place to start to change old, ingrained beliefs is to challenge them by asking yourself a simple question. Do the beliefs I have serve me in a way that helps me grow and learn, or do I hold onto some limiting beliefs about myself that hold me back? Our minds will only process the relevant information it needs at the time and then make sweeping generalisations each time it experiences those things to confirm what is already believed.

Beliefs determine to some extent what we will pay attention to, focus on, notice and pull into our awareness. Every other piece of information that passes through the processing system of our brains is then deleted and classed as being irrelevant.

For example, if a person who is creating amazing success in their business believes they're great at business and wants to keep getting better, they will look for ways to confirm that belief and continue to improve to the exclusion of everything that limits their success. If I truly believe I am awesome at what I do, my actions will naturally follow suit to confirm that belief. So the saying, 'fake it 'til you make it' kind of applies here too and is not a bad mantra to have initially, until those beliefs become embedded and confirmed. Imagine what would happen if a business owner believed they were terrible at business instead. They would then start noticing all the things to confirm *that* belief and as a result their business would not succeed.

Think about your own life and what you've decided is true for yourself. The point is to see if you are holding onto any limiting beliefs or if the beliefs you have about yourself serve and aid your growth and development in life. Try asking yourself if the beliefs you have limit your potential or do they serve and empower you for your future self? Whatever we decide to believe is true about ourselves, our actions will follow suit. We can alter the state of our current situation if we start believing in ourselves enough to want more from life. When we start doing that, new actions and new habits will form and our world begins to change in a positive way. We just have to start believing it first.

Values

So where do we begin? The foundations are partly formed by values installed in us by our family and friends. According to the Collins dictionary, values are: *the value of something such as a quality, attitude or method is its importance or usefulness. If you place a particular value on something, that is the importance or usefulness you think it has. The moral principles and beliefs or accepted standards of a person or social group.*

Values guide our every decision whether we are consciously aware of it or not. A large factor in determining our values is the family environment, but also those close to us that become part of our inner circle. They subconsciously impart some of their values as well as a natural by-product of being around them. When you know what is most important to you making decisions is effortless. Values are what we stand for and more often than not, we seek out others who have similar values to our own as a source of comfort and security – like attracts like; whether it's beneficial or not, we are drawn to others who value the same things as we do. Values determine our level of happiness and we naturally want to experience the positive benefits of them, as they reinforce those deep-seated qualities we have linked to our core identity.

When you know what is most important to you making a decision is easy. But how many of us have taken the time to find out what our values are? How many of us have examined them to see if they help serve what we believe to be true about ourselves, or are they in conflict and leading us to feel frustrated, angry, lost and confused? Are we able to make those decisions without a second thought, or is there an underlining feeling that makes making a decision hard when it seems to conflict with our core values?

For example, if someone within your inner circle, those of influence, asked you to steal something from the local store to prove your commitment to the group, would you be able to make that decision without a second thought? Would that make you feel uneasy? Is stealing the item in conflict with your innate core values of trustworthiness, honesty and integrity? If a feeling of uneasiness occurs of it 'not feeling right', then this is a very good indication that conflict is occurring. The act of stealing that item goes against a strong value of yours. If you've ever found yourself in a situation where it was tough to make a decision, the reason is probably that you were unclear about what you valued most within that situation.

Was it staying true to yourself or was it trying to show your commitment level to the group?

Values can include things such as health, vitality, integrity, joy, connection, passion, creativity, happiness, achievement, growth and much more. Remember, when you know what is important to you making a decision and acting in accordance with those values becomes easy. Knowing what your core values are, allows you to maintain your focus on your goals without being distracted by frivolous, unimportant things that have no meaning, like watching television endlessly day after day. It serves only to stagnate the mind and is a time-wasting activity that steers you off course from what you truly desire to do. It has no meaning or purpose whatsoever. If something has no meaning what's the point in doing it?

To achieve long-lasting happiness, we need to live congruently with our values – our highest ideals. To do this, we must be clear about what our values are and yet many people aren't clear but confused. They go through life, wondering why they're not happy, not feeling sustained or purpose-filled, but lonely, isolated, sad and even depressed. These feelings often boil over into frustration, or 'what's the point of doing anything' type sentiments and angry at the world because life has dished them up a bad deal. These feelings spiral out of control and manifest themselves into anti-social behaviour and a feeling of regret later in life. These people have no idea who they are, who they want to be or how they even want to feel. They live their lives reacting to events around them hoping and wishing that it will all work out in the long run without taking any responsibility for themselves. It doesn't work like that.

Some people have a fair idea of knowing what they want to have – more time, more money, love, health and so on, without ever knowing who they want to be. All they know is, they want more and because they haven't identified what is important to them, including what they value, they wander around without a clear sense of direction of *how* to achieve long-term happiness and success. Most, therefore, give up resigning themselves to living a life that's less than fulfilling and feeling victimised because things didn't work out the way they wanted them to. They continue to be stuck in a rut looking forward to the weekend and dreading Monday morning. This is not long-lasting fulfilment. This is a classic example of just going through the motions and not feeling satisfied internally.

It's easy to forget about what's important to you, about your core values, when there's a decision to be made that would mean a personal challenge for you. If you want to know what it feels like to not live congruently with who you are and what you believe in, make a decision that doesn't keep your values intact. What inevitably happens is an internal uneasiness arises and problems keep re-occurring, like the example I gave about stealing the item from the shop. You'll never look back on that incident with pride because you traded your values for the easy ride to fit in with the in-crowd. However, you will always remember those times you chose to live according to your values, with who you are and what you believe in, especially if there is a personal cost to you. This may be in the form of time, effort or saying no when it would be easier to say yes. These moments are when we feel proud for all the *right* reasons.

I'd encourage you to do the following activity and ask yourself, what feelings do I want to experience so that I know I am being true to myself? A great starting point is to think of moments when you felt truly fulfilled. What were you doing? Describe how you felt. When we can identify what makes us feel pleasure and fulfilment, we can go about creating that for ourselves each day. Being aware of what's important to us, allows us to choose to focus on highlighting those values that give us that inner sense of peace and satisfaction. Take a moment to think about what values are important to you. Challenge yourself to think about them and then write a list of them. What are your values?

We all have certain expectations about what has to happen for us to feel our values are being met. For example, one of my highest values is personal integrity. I place a great deal of emphasis on this value being met in whatever I do. It means that whoever I have dealings with, it needs to be a win for me and a win for them. In other words, it has to be mutually beneficial for both parties so neither party walks away feeling at a loss or that one has won at the expense of the other. It also means that every person speaks their truth, that no-one lies and that it's okay to have a difference of opinion, as long as the space in which those opinions are raised is respected.

This means that we listen with the intent to understand, that we listen to one another's concerns, that we are able to explain what other's points of view may be and come to a mutually beneficial agreement, where all parties feel valued and heard. The only way this is met is through a win-win environment that values what others have to say and shows a genuine interest in them. The best outcomes are those where every person feels valued and personal integrity remains not only intact, but is validated and respected.

Respect

"Respect your efforts, respect yourself. Self-respect leads to self-discipline. When you have both firmly under your belt, that's real power."

Clint Eastwood

It's interesting that in this age of technology where life is supposedly made easier because of the convenience of online shopping, human beings seem to have lost the art of connection with one another. More importantly, they've lost it with themselves. It seems this age has created more problems than solutions, difficulty instead of ease and a serious lack of personal growth and development skills that would enable people to function easily within society.

The education system is subjectively designed at the medium intelligence level of children, whilst those that are either struggling or highly intelligent are not typically catered for in mainstream classrooms. This issue combined with the demands of having to be technologically savvy, has created a generation that don't have the necessary life skills to enable them to overcome and deal with negative, stressful or challenging situations. They simply do not have the skills.

The system hasn't catered for them properly in what I deem to be the most fundamental skill development necessary – life skills. It's a serious issue that sees a lot of young adults struggling to budget, struggling to prioritise, battling to pay their rent or to save money for a home and have very little idea how to achieve their full potential in their lives. That's why this age has also seen a huge rise in life coaches, counsellors and advisors, to help undo some of the damage that has already been done in family units, friendship circles, the school environment or other significant influences, that have contributed to this issue of being under-skilled or damaged psychologically.

Starting with the very fundamentals of respect, I felt it necessary to include and delve a little deeper into the area, to help develop a deeper understanding of it in its various forms and its applications in life. Without this fundamental core value being explored further, it's pointless looking at other traits without developing a deeper understanding of what respect is first. Respect forms the basis of all relationships whether family, friends, acquaintances or strangers and it's important to understand it thoroughly.

For this book the main focus is on self-respect and respect for others, however, it is important to understand there are other types of respect as well. Many believe that respect is earned whilst others believe it is automatically expected when we interact with ourselves and others. Comments such as, 'Don't you have any self-respect?' or 'Show some respect' get thrown around a lot and it can make us question ourselves and whether we do have it. But why is respect so important in the first place?

Respect is a naturally occurring feeling that human beings have. Respect isn't about controlling someone or making them do what you want them to do. Respect is about the freedom to be yourself and to be loved for who you are. It doesn't matter what race, religion, creed or colour you are, when you walk out your front door each day as you undertake your daily tasks and routines, you know you want to look your best and present yourself in the best possible manner.

Imagine walking out your front door in a dirty old t-shirt, ripped jeans and not showered to go to work and then expecting others to respect how you look. One would conclude that your level of self-respect is quite low, which in turn affects how you behave and interact with others (most likely poorly). How we present ourselves to others is a reflection of how much we value ourselves, how much we respect our workplaces and their requirements. As a result of presenting yourself poorly, relationships may become strained and your confidence levels drop. This could have easily been avoided by complying with the dress code.

We show respect through certain gestures like handshakes or being polite to others and using assertive body language skills (more on assertiveness later). Respecting someone doesn't mean you worship the ground they walk on, it's treating people in a dignified, courteous manner. This principle also applies to ourselves which at times some of us forget to do. Sometimes we don't treat ourselves with the same dignity and consideration as we do to others which seems quite ironic. We want respect, we expect it, but sometimes we aren't respecting ourselves enough to know we deserve better.

In some cultures, respect is earned. You respect someone if they treat you right first or if they do something worthy of respect. For example, when a person does a good deed not seeking the praises of others or have accomplished greatness in whatever form that is in their life. A great example of this is Nelson Mandela. He stood up against his own corrupt political leaders of South Africa, was jailed for twenty-seven years in isolation and upon his release from jail, ended up becoming one of the greatest leaders South Africa had ever seen. A man that is worthy of respect.

Respect is an innate quality we seem to automatically and naturally have an awareness of. Generation after generation respect is probably the number one quality taught and insisted upon in every family around the globe. Outwardly, it is expected to show itself by behaving in acceptable ways, by adhering to the laws of the land, the local rules and regulations and of course within the home itself. We have respect for things, the way we handle and use our mobile phones for example, so why is it that some don't respect themselves enough to know that they are worthy of more? Worthy of love, of achieving greatness, having wonderful relationships and not being bound by others expectations of them and living a happy and productive life. Respect forms the basis of every interaction we have. It has different meanings to different people, but generally people understand the meaning of it and its application.

Like many, I grew up being told to respect my elders. I was recently speaking with my neighbour who attended the funeral of an elderly friend of the family. Whilst talking with two of the guests he had known since he was a child, he addressed them as Mr and Mrs. He too, had been told to do this by his parents and until he was invited to address them both by their given name, he addressed them using Mr and Mrs. It was an unwritten rule that when you address others who are older than you, your parents' age or older, you address them by their surname. Sadly, this practice has declined with the digital age and it makes me wonder if some ever learned what respect is. Did they have the necessary skills to apply respect in any given situation? If it isn't being implemented consistently in the family environment or being taught in personal growth and development programs, then how are young people supposed to know all the accepted levels of behaviour? How are they to reach their full potential without knowing this?

Individuals who have been immersed in home environments that have been of poor standard with inconsistent consequences for breaking home rules, have come through to adulthood with major hang-ups and behavioural or psychological issues. The damage has already been done. Now living sub-standard, unfulfilled lives, they start to see others around them achieving success and wonder how they did it. They start believing that they are worthy of more than their current conditions dictate, but often have no idea where to even begin.

There are different levels of dysfunctional, unconscious thinking and likewise different levels of functional thinking. Each category of behaviour has its resultant behaviours or actions that are seen outwardly. Firstly, relying on others in a dysfunctional, unhealthy manner manifests itself typically by blaming others, focusing only on the problem at hand, having an attitude whereby 'the world owes me a favour' and people who exhibit such behaviours won't make decisions for themselves. They'll say things like, 'I can't because…' which is really saying, 'I am not mature enough, nor do I want to take responsibility for my actions because I have other people to rely on to do it for me'. It's a disempowering level of thinking where an individual may get trapped if they don't recognise that they need to grow up and start making decisions that will help move them forward in life. It can also manifest itself in behaviours that appear anti-social and disrespectful by nature as well.

The next stage is the rebellious stage, which again in a dysfunctional way does not serve the individual. The signs of this stage are that they are argumentative, act in a self-righteous and/or rebellious way and they can't see an optimistic future for themselves. It's a toxic stage with no positive outcomes at all. Those primarily affected by people in this stage are not only the individual themselves, but loved ones such as family members who cop the brunt of outbursts of unacceptable behaviours.

If a parent for example, had chosen a good college for their child to attend, had paid for tuition and perhaps decided what field of interest their son/daughter would go into, someone in the rebellious stage would refuse to go to the college, not attend the course and decide that they don't need a university degree to get a good education. They may decide to travel the world and go backpacking instead. It manifests itself in outlandish behaviours, that can also affect loved ones quite dramatically, if no responsibility for self is taken.

The expected outcomes that individuals get as a result of the above-mentioned thinking patterns and behaviours are that they undervalue themselves and eventually have the victim mentality. Individuals in these stages are treading down a very dangerous path if they don't recognise the warning signs. As expected, the outward manifestations of these types of patterns result in anti-social behaviour, addiction issues, self-destructive patterns, don't contribute to society healthily and productively and don't find happiness and long-lasting, sustaining relationships. They often end up on support payments of some description and go through life unfulfilled, outwardly reflecting a lack of self-worth in the way they behave. The lack of responsibility, lack of skill development and further education all contributes to a person feeling disempowered and outwardly acting out. They do not have the necessary skills or confidence levels to understand how to behave properly, how to be contributing members of society and how to ultimately chase and fulfil their life's dream. It's a sad reality that many in the technological and digital age find themselves so disempowered, disconnected and undervalued, that a society that is supposed to be made easier by the addition of the world wide web, has inadvertently made things harder.

If those at this end of the scale keep progressing down that self-destructive path, the realisation they can get to is that their life 'sucks' and conclude – what's the point of life anyway. Those at this end of the spectrum are in danger of suicidal tendencies (which is a cry for help) and at worst can result in death. They have no idea what to do, where to go or how to escape the nightmare they have found themselves in. Interestingly enough, they truly believe that it has all just happened *to* them, that none of it was their fault, none of it they chose, it just happened that way. Individuals at this end are in real danger. Self-respect has evaded them.

On the flip side, there are different levels of functional thinking and the results depend on where they are at on the scale. Again, the first stage is to rely on others, but in a way that helps them move forward. This is a sign of growth and maturity, as asking for help means they believe in themselves enough to want more – they just don't know how to attain their aspirations yet. In the beginning, once someone has been able to reach out and ask for help, they can then put together a plan of action so that each day becomes productive and not self-destructive anymore. It can start by looking at role models and asking those educated in their field how they did it. It may then involve modelling those people, reading books about others who've made it, trusting a system that works and implementing those systems for themselves. Their level of self-respect is rising.

As confidence grows, people at this stage start getting that self-belief back and begin to make empowering decisions, begin challenging the nagging doubts and slowly begin changing their circumstances. This may mean excluding certain people from their lives that have only served to keep them stuck in a rut and widening their circle of influence to include those people who will challenge them, who will have interesting conversations with them and help them along the road of self-discovery. They begin to distance themselves from their past, the situation they've found themselves caught in and realise they are worthy of more.

As expected, the results are much more positive, much more empowering and their perspective about themselves, their situation and what they want in life begins to shift. Their ability to achieve positive outcomes increases and their emotional intelligence levels are now developing and improving. They are now 'owning' their situation, realising that the way they have been living their lives hasn't been serving them well, hasn't been productive and there is much more to life than staring at a television for twenty-four hours a day and swearing at their parents because they didn't do their washing for them! They are finally taking responsibility for themselves and like a light bulb switches on, it dawns on them that the only person responsible for how things are – are themselves. It isn't Mum or Dad's fault, it isn't the fact they divorced when they were a child, it isn't the fact that the neighbourhood in which they were raised was of low socioeconomic standing. It was because they were in complete denial, immature, irresponsible and too scared to take ownership of their own lives. It isn't anyone else's fault of how things are now – it is theirs. Finally, they realise that they can do more and they have so many opportunities waiting for them if they choose to take them. At this level their perspective has now shifted, new and helpful relationships are developing as a result of their new-found self-belief and an action plan is being implemented consistently to achieve their goals in life.

The ultimate achievement is to realise they are now living their dream. They have gotten off the lounge room chair, they're being proactive in their choices, have now developed their circle of influence to include those who will aid them in their quest for more and surround themselves with people who are highly emotionally intelligent. They choose to be with people who are wise and discerning, who have integrity and who are successful people in all facets of their lives.

This final stage is where we all aim to be – achieving goals we set for ourselves, to learn from the mistakes of the past and moving forward every day to bettering ourselves. It's when we realise we are worthy of more that we achieve more. It's by those positive actions, of being aware of how we manage and use our time, of taking full responsibility and ownership of all our behaviours and initiating change, that we achieve our unique purpose in life – whatever that may be. It is here that a person becomes a highly functioning human being, contributing to society as a whole and whose own self-confidence and emotional intelligence is at its optimal peak. This is where every human being deserves to be.

Respecting yourself enough to believe that is critical. It opens the doors to possibilities and opportunities to present themselves when you do. Understanding all about respect and its various applications puts you ahead of the pack. You understand it underpins every interaction you have in life and that's definitely an advantage.

Tool 2

The difference between proactive and reactive people

"Being successful requires being proactive and not waiting for life to come to you. It means you're on offence, not defence. You're active, not passive."

Benjamin P. Hardy

It's important to understand the difference between being proactive and reactive, how these each influence our lives and how they become relevant and influential to every decision we make and every action we take. There is a major difference between the two, and how a person experiences their life depends upon whether they are being proactive or reactive. How we can create our world (our maps), depends upon whether we are deciding to make empowering and beneficial decisions that will propel us forward, or whether we are merely reacting to situations and believing that life just happens and there's nothing that can be done to change things. Reactive people will experience sporadic, inconsistent results with no real vision for their future selves, continuing old patterns of behaviour and keeping them stuck where they are.

Proactivity involves more than just taking initiative; it means we take responsibility for our own lives. How we behave is a function of each decision we make. It is not a result of things happening in our lives that determine things, it is the choices we make that do. How we choose to respond to situations, to other people, our circumstances, to every event we experience, will then determine whether or not we are being proactive or reactive.

| WHAT HAPPENED? EVENT ISSUE | → | CHOICE RESPONSIBILITY MATURITY | → | RESPONSE OUTCOME |

The above diagram adapted from Stephen Covey's model, *The Seven Habits of Highly Effective People* shows that between the event and the outcome, lies the freedom to choose how we respond to every situation. The word responsibility is a combination of two words – *response* and *able* indicating we can respond to situations in a way we choose. Each of these choices has an outcome; whether that outcome is positive and assertive or not, depends upon the response given in that moment. Was it based on your feelings, how you felt in that moment? Or was it based on deep-seated values and a strong sense of self?

A proactive person is not a slave to their feelings, but rather is value-driven. They are highly emotionally intelligent and therefore can control how they respond to events. Their feelings and emotions don't dictate and determine how they respond, as they've developed the maturity to make their feelings subordinate to their logic. They choose and control how they respond. Their feelings don't determine their actions; their deep-seated values do. A proactive person sees every event, every encounter in a positive way and their self-esteem is not influenced by outside sources or circumstances. It doesn't matter if it is cold, miserable and wet, it doesn't matter if something someone says to them is negative. It doesn't affect how they feel about themselves.

Because proactive people have core values such as integrity and trust, outside influences do not affect their level of self-confidence or their ability to act in a manner that is mature and responsible. They don't simply react to situations they find themselves in, choosing to determine their response, rather than allowing themselves to be affected by others outward behaviours. Proactive people have built their confidence levels to hinge upon their core values and self-belief and not upon the influences in their environment that can affect their performance.

On the other hand, a reactive person believes that life just happens to them, that it's other people's fault that things are the way they are, that they haven't had a choice when a situation has gone wrong, that circumstances have determined why they are where they are right now. Reactive people are highly influenced by outside sources and their self-confidence is dependent upon what others think about them. It wavers between being high and low and anywhere in-between, depending upon whether the feedback they receive is positive or negative. It has a major impact on the decisions they make (or lack thereof), that they're bound by circumstances and are a victim in the grand scheme of things.

Reactive people typically say phrases like, 'Things like that always happens to me' or 'I didn't have a choice, I had to' and firmly believe that they are the victim in circumstances they find themselves in. They cannot see they have choices and that those choices create the circumstances they find themselves in. They feel burdened by the weight of responsibility they carry of other people's problems and circumstances, leaving little or no time to focus on their own wants and needs in life.

Even though we cannot control all situations, I believe that it's the responsibility of us all to respond in a way that not only serves us, but also helps those we choose to interact with. A win-win scenario is the ideal outcome. Circumstances should never determine us – we determine them. In other words, it is our responsibility to *choose* to act wisely, maturely and in a responsible, proactive way if our goals in life are to be achieved. If you want to feel empowered, strong, confident and able, then you need to start making proactive decisions and then act upon them. To do nothing is action as well.

Let's say you recently passed a course in Hospitality. It is wonderful that you made the decision to further yourself and get educated and qualified, but what happens next determines how you'll experience your world. Does the certificate stay hung up on the wall as something to be admired and that's it? The map you create next will be determined by whether you make a proactive choice that serves to propel you towards your goal of working in the industry, or whether you decide to sit back and admire the certificate on the wall and do nothing about it. Are you going to wait for 'just the right time' to get work, reacting to circumstances like it being off-season and not being busy enough to warrant looking for work? This is procrastination at its best. When we get comfortable with the excuses again to justify our lack of motivation, we in effect determine the outcome of not being gainfully employed, versus being proactive and taking the resume with the certificate and looking for work. Two very different outcomes and each determined by whether the decisions that were made in each moment has served and empowered or a result of reacting to circumstances. It is the responsibility and the freedom to choose how we respond to each event, to each stimulus, that determines the outcome we get.

I know at times my health becomes the most pressing event in my life and it seems at times that circumstances dictate the response I give to each intensely painful episode of sickness. It's in these moments that my character traits are put to the test. Am I a proactive person who takes the lead mentally to decide what outcome I want or do I curl up and feel like I am a victim of my circumstances and let the world pass me by? There are times when I do not have the energy or feel well enough to do the things I want to do and I can accept that. In those moments when the pain becomes intense, I won't give in to the temptation of feeling sorry for myself, thinking I have it harder than others and do nothing. I know I'm worth more than allowing pain to dictate the terms of my life.

So how does a person who has lived in reactive mode become proactive? The issue for many is they seek a quick and simple way to solve the issues they are facing and again think that the issue is 'out there' and not from within. Statements like 'There's nothing I can do to change things – it is what it is' indicate a person is living in reactive mode. They are not taking control, not making responsible decisions and choices, that help transform their lives into one that will be fulfilling. Again, the problem is 'out there' that stuff just happens and there is no responsibility in these statements. There's no responsibility for the outcomes they get and no proactive action taken either. Is it any wonder so many are feeling powerless, miserable and not sustained?

Experts tell us it takes consistent effort for new habits to form and to create change. It starts with one step at a time. In my workshops, when participants are hungry for a new and improved version of themselves, I remind them of this fact because it isn't instantaneous – it takes time and patience. The road ahead is full of hurdles that a person must be willing to overcome, to walk over some inconsistently paved walkways and build that resilience. Because you are changing lifelong habits, changing how you do things, how you view things, how you react to situations and events, you will find that some people will criticise you, judge you and question you, as to why you're being the way you are. Those closest to you that aren't supporting your quest for a better you, will drop off along the way and you need to recognise that this is going to happen. It's a natural part of the process. It doesn't mean you're being a mean person and that you should feel guilty as some will undoubtedly say, but it is now your responsibility to choose to let these people go, to not continue to spend time with people who do not challenge and support you.

Eleanor Roosevelt once famously said, "No one can make you feel inferior without your consent" and this is a tactic some people will try to use to undermine you. Be aware that others do not have that power over you unless you choose to give it to them. Having this awareness is a positive step forward in creating transformation. People like this with hidden agendas, who are driven by envy and insecurity, need to be out of your life, if you seek the transformation you so richly deserve. It all starts with consciously deciding to be proactive in every moment and not just reacting anymore.

It's through deep self-reflection and being honest and raw with yourself that true transformation occurs. It is a process – a lifelong journey, where positive change is inevitable if a person decides they want it. Remember, between the event and the outcome lies the freedom to choose how you respond and that choice lies with you and you only. Only you can create the change you seek. The power lies with you. The question to ask yourself is which side of the equation are you on right now? Are you the type of person who is the cause of the things that happen in your life or are you at the effect side of things that happen to you? Do you make things happen by showing initiative, creativity, commitment and drive or do you merely react to situations you find yourself in? How you respond to these questions will give a very good indication of where things are for you right now.

Between the stimulus and response is the critical point. It's where the power of choice lies. It's where we can create long-lasting change that will help us grow or where we can decide to be living in reaction only. We are either at the effect side of the equation or the cause side. We are either causing (or deciding) something to happen or we are experiencing the effects of it. Even doing nothing is a conscious choice and it is at the cause end. You've decided to do nothing. If, however, when you've had nothing to do you made the decision to go for a walk or read a book, the outcome you would have reaped would have benefited you. You determined the outcome by choosing to respond to the situation in a positive way instead.

All actions have an effect whether they serve us or whether they don't. To help a person become proactive, it is more than showing initiative. It is choosing responsibly. It's deciding that in every moment when there's a decision to be made, even a simple one like choosing between McDonald's or a salad sandwich, whether your decisions are going to serve you or not. Are they going to give you the outcomes you desire? By choosing McDonald's over a salad sandwich are you going to get the desired outcome of better health and aid your weight loss goals? If you chose the salad sandwich option, it would aid your aspirations and have other beneficial effects on your mind and body as well. Again, the choice at that moment lies solely with you and you reap the benefits (or repercussions) of each decision you make.

Being at cause, learning to be proactive, really means we are taking action that benefits us in a way that we are learning and growing. If we are at the effect (or reactive) end of the spectrum, we are simply reacting to situations that happen and not taking meaningful action that helps us. The issue for many who are at the reactive end, is that their self-esteem is so low, that they feel that they aren't good enough, intelligent enough, don't have the resources or opportunities other people have and therefore fall victim to their circumstances. It's a trap that's cyclic and by becoming aware, by getting further educated, by learning new and better ways of doing things, a person can start to recognise the signs and take responsibility for their lives positively and proactively.

Reactive people blame their environment, blame their parents, blame others for how bad things are and the situation they find themselves in. Reactive people deflect responsibility, lack maturity and understanding, whilst the opposite is true of proactive people. Remember to create long-lasting change, to change years of conditioning and form new habits, you need to stick with it for a minimum of thirty days to create lasting change.

Reactive Language	Proactive Language
There's nothing I can do.	Let's look at alternatives.
That's just the way I am.	I can choose a different approach.
He makes me so mad.	I control my feelings.
They won't allow that.	I can ask for alternatives.
I have to do that.	I can choose to do that.
I can't.	I won't/I choose not to.
I must.	I prefer/I'd like to.
If only.	I will.

The table shows the difference between reactive and proactive language. How we language things creates our world and our paradigms (or maps) and are then influenced by what we say.

Let's take the first example, 'There's nothing I can do' as opposed to 'Let's look at alternatives'. Two very different worlds are created by what they have said yet the facts of the matter are the same. There's an issue around a clear direction to be taken and the reactive person typically says that nothing can be done about it, thus abrogating responsibility altogether. There's no ownership. It reflects an immature and underdeveloped resource base and therefore, the problem of what to do about the issue remains the same.

On the flip side, the proactive person realises that the issue of what to do about the problem needs solving and instead of using reactive language, demonstrates proactive language by seeking out alternatives. They realise the issue needs to be dealt with regardless of what seems unsolvable at the moment, but their level of maturity, level of resources they have internally, allows them to dictate the circumstances. In other words, they find solutions to problems.

As the examples indicate, what we verbalise creates the world in which we live and how successfully or unsuccessfully we will experience it as well. Words are powerful and create significant meaning and attachments, so becoming aware of what words you choose to use is another step that can be taken to help improve yourself and start learning to be more proactive.

Regardless of whether our beliefs support us to believe we are worthy of change or not is irrelevant at this point, because believing we can make things happen, believing we can start being proactive instead of reactive, helps begin the process of positive change in our lives. If you don't believe it's true yet, act as if it is – pretend. At this stage, believing it to be true will then help determine what steps you take to empower yourself, what decisions you make in each moment and what experiences you will create as a result. The rest will be filtered out as irrelevant and you'll start creating a new set of circumstances, one in which you've proactively made decisions and taken responsibility for yourself, instead of giving reasons why things didn't work out for you.

If someone believes they are not at cause for anything in their life, even though they haven't looked for a job and they spend all their time blaming others for their bad luck, they are going to experience a certain type of world. Compare this experience to someone who believes that they are at cause. They will find a way to work. They won't blame, they will take responsibility and will be proactive in changing the circumstances of their life as well. Compare this with people on the effect side of things who go through life with reasons. Reasons why things didn't work out as well as they hoped for. Hoping for anything does nothing to create change. There's no action in these words. There's no *doing* only being. At this point, we need action words and not wishy-washy statements that have no accountability attached to them.

People who go through life on the effect side of the equation have reasons. They'll be able to tell you why they are not successful and why something hasn't worked out. 'It was because my ex-wife didn't support me', 'I didn't get the breaks I deserved', 'The school I went to didn't have a great curriculum', 'My boss is hard to work for'. They have reasons or justifications why they didn't get promoted, why they aren't internally happy and yet take little or no responsibility for the predicament they find themselves in. Perhaps some of the reasons they give are true and contribute to the issue at hand, but unless a person who finds themselves in this situation realises that it is all within them to change their circumstances, to change how they respond to situations – nothing will change.

This begs the question then. How satisfying is the life they are currently leading? How much joy, courage, love, empowerment or resourcefulness can someone feel if they live with their stories – with the reasons why they can't? Better yet, why are they choosing *not* to succeed, choosing *not* to take responsibility for change, because a person who says, 'I can't' is really saying 'I choose not to.'

Questions for you:

1. Are you reacting to your circumstances and not living up to your potential?

2. What type of language do you primarily use?

3. How can you be more proactive to improve the quality of your life?

Tool 3

What you focus on is what you get

"Always remember, your focus determines your reality."

George Lucas

Have you ever heard of the saying, 'what you focus on is what you get?' Not a truer word has been spoken. Unfortunately, when we focus on negative issues they tend to manifest and grow to the exclusion of all else.

The mind is a powerful tool and can help us lead happy and productive lives or the flip is also true. For example, problem-focused people who only see issues without finding answers to those problems, tend to go round and round in circles and this leads to unnecessary anxiety. Problem-focused people have trouble switching off their brain and tend to go to bed at night thinking about all the problems they have, which can lead to sleep deprivation and mood disorders. It becomes their reality. If a person is focusing on the problem and not on finding solutions, the problem grows and grows and becomes overwhelming and all-consuming.

People who are problem-focused who sit and think about the problems they have, talking about only their issues with others and then journal about them are excluding all other possibilities. The problem which may have started as a small issue has now grown in intensity, leaving the person feeling powerless and out of control. By airing the problems on social media, you are in actuality, giving the problem an unnecessary voice. The likes and comments that follow suit only go to affirm that you're justified in feeling anxious, feeling down and depressed and therefore, it's okay to keep repeating these patterns of behaviour. You've been validated and being validated is a natural human need.

Whether the need is being met positively or negatively, either way the need is met. In this case, when someone is posting about how bad things are and getting rewarded for it, people are inadvertently reinforcing that negative mindset. Those who are liking and commenting and showing pity and sympathy are then enabling that individual and suddenly they feel justified, almost entitled to feel the way they do and so the pattern of misery continues. If the pattern continues, no positive change will occur. It can't because all other options have been excluded and the validation that was sought has been upheld by the likes and comments. You only need to look at a person's social media account to get a glimpse at their mindset. Are they posting about their issues or posting something to indicate there is a problem going on? Check it out, read between the lines and you will find what I'm saying is true. A person's social media account is often a gateway into the level of happiness and contentment they have in life.

The same is true for the content of your conversations with others. Do you talk only about how bad things are or how the situation you've found yourself in really sucks and there is nothing you can do about it? Or are you having robust conversations, stimulating, relevant conversations that are not problem-focused but are solution-focused? If there are issues that need resolving, acknowledge there's a problem, but find solutions to the problem at hand. It may take extra effort, it may take thinking and writing about alternatives to the issue and seeking help from others, but you've now become solution-focused and *not* problem-focused. A major shift in thinking has resulted.

The same is true for journaling. I've always encouraged my clients to keep a journal, but it's had some stipulations around what my client writes about. I'm not saying to not acknowledge there's a problem – not at all. But unless a person has either learned a lesson from the actions they took to address the issue or are writing about alternatives to solve the problem, then what's the point in writing about them? If you're writing about them for the sake of writing about them, then the problem will grow. This will leave you feeling weighed down, powerless and victimised. It is problem-focused.

So instead of focusing on problems write about things you're grateful for. This is a great technique for shifting the mindset of a person to one of hope and opportunity instead of feeling powerless and out of control. Write about things you take for granted each day, that you naturally assume will happen. For example, as I am writing now, I can hear birds singing, the sun is shining and the sky is a pale blue colour. It's peaceful and quiet. I have uninterrupted time to write. I have my needs met like food in the fridge and a bed to sleep in and on it goes. If my focus takes a one-eighty turn and I am not thinking, talking or writing about the problems I have, I don't have the time I had previously to devote to them. My focus is now changing and the light of hope and gratitude begins to fill the space instead. The idea behind writing about what you're grateful for, is to shift that focus from being problem-centred and feeling powerless, to one of empowerment. When we feel empowered, we tend to look for solutions rather than focusing on problems. It's a great starting point. By giving gratitude a voice you are now silencing the issues that once consumed you and shifting your focus elsewhere.

It's like when you or someone you care about suddenly gets ill. It seems only natural to take your health for granted, that you'll always have a reasonable amount of healthiness and independence until it's taken away. I call it the 'Gr rule' – what we take for granted is what we need to be grateful for (more on this later in the book). A powerful way to adjust your thinking patterns is to begin giving gratitude air, to begin writing about gratitude in those journals and posting on social media the positive elements of your life and watch how the problem's size diminishes. Its intensity dies down and a feeling of control returns. Sleep patterns suddenly begin changing for the better, the level of anxiety over issues reduces and possibilities for solutions begin to present themselves. If a person is problem-focused, all they get are never-ending problems without any viable solutions.

Along with these indicators are colours. Colours play an important part in how a person feels as well. Again, taking social media as an example, if a person posts a problem and the background is black, guaranteed there will be no positive outcome to that post and it's a strong indicator of how a person is feeling. On the opposite side of the coin is a person who has a similar problem, but posts about a positive outcome they experienced and not the problem itself. The background colour chosen will be brighter and more cheerful as well. Again, it reflects where that person is at in life, their level of happiness and self-fulfilment, because they were able to tap into resources and find solutions to the problem. Two very different viewpoints and quite a contrast with how they've chosen to react to the same situation.

Have you ever heard of the analogy of the glass half empty and the glass half full? I'm sure you have at some point in time and it's a great indicator of a person's focus as well. People who are problem-focused will look at a glass and say it is half empty. People who are proactive, have a sterling attitude of gratitude and who are solution-focused, will see it as half full. It's the same glass of water, but the mindset of the individual will determine how they see that glass of water.

Another way to illustrate this point of focus is to use an example I came across. The first picture is of a boy holding one piece of cake and the other is of a boy holding the entire cake but with a piece missing. Now the boy with the one piece of cake is beaming and happy. He is looking at his singular piece of cake and is grateful for it. He may be admiring the thick icing on the top, the creaminess of the cream and the sweetness of the jam in the centre and how the sponge looks light and fluffy. He may even appreciate the hands that made it as well. But his focus is purely on the piece he does have and not on what he doesn't have. He feels an overwhelming sense of gratitude.

In the second picture, the boy is holding an entire cake and only a piece missing and he looks miserable. His face shows sadness because the cake he is holding in his hands has a piece missing out of it. His focus is not on the cake he is holding but on the piece that is missing. He feels wronged, feels cheated almost because the cake wasn't full and begins questioning why. Where has that missing piece gone? Who took that piece and why did they take it? Why haven't I got all of the cake? The relentless questions he raises and the statements he vocalises about what he *doesn't* have, creates problem after problem and his lack of appreciation for the cake he's holding goes unnoticed. His focus on the missing piece causes unnecessary stress and anxiety and upsets others around him causing avoidable problems, because he chose to focus on what was missing. He chose not to be grateful for what he had which was almost an entire cake in his hands.

What we focus on is what we get. If we focus on what we have, what we are grateful for, that gratitude grows and a deeper sense of appreciation develops. If we are focused on what we don't have, we miss out on opportunities and create unnecessary stress and worry and problems that once didn't exist. To illustrate the point of what we focus on is what we get and what that means for us, we need to delve a little deeper, particularly if your focus has been a little 'off' lately. As the above example illustrates, what we focus on is what we will find evidence for to the exclusion of everything else. Two boys had cake. Two boys had two different focus points and both were to the exclusion of all else. Whether that was helpful or not that's what they did.

Our reality is only what we perceive and we only perceive what we focus on. Think of a torch and the light it projects. What the light shines on is where the focus is. What's outside that light are possibilities. Now whether those possibilities are applicable or not, you won't know unless you start expanding the light and the realms of possibilities to include those aspects where the torch hasn't yet been shining. Our lives and how we experience our world are the same thing. We won't be aware of things beyond our focus if we aren't willing and able to expand that light and delve into unknown possibilities to explore options. Exploration means delving into unknown territory and unknown territory is where fear often lies.

If we focus on something and it causes us to feel fear, what we can't experience is appreciation. To focus on our fear is to exclude what we are capable of and what a disservice to oneself that is. The solution is to focus on feeling appreciation even if it feels uncomfortable, new and strange and learn to disassociate fear from the unknown in those areas outside the torch's focus. When we tap into that emotion of appreciation, of feeling gratitude, the fear we had built and manifested within ourselves fades. It dissipates.

It takes lots of practice to push aside the doubtful self-talk, but over time it becomes natural to feel appreciation and gratitude when you experience a new event. You've shifted your focus and the associations you had to include things you hadn't considered and whether or not the answers you were seeking were found on the first, second or third go, the point is you went looking. You expanded the torch's light by pushing your comfort zone and that's commendable. It takes courage to do these things and courage and fear cannot co-exist in the same space. By being courageous, you're now diminishing the power of fear and empowerment and positivity reign at the possibility of new learnings, new focus points and ones that will serve you in your journey through life.

Tool 4

⊃━━⊂

Finding purpose and meaning

"When you find your purpose, it is like your heart has been set alight with passion. You know it absolutely, without any doubt."
Rhonda Byrne

Tony Robbins, the famous American life coach, entrepreneur and business owner grew up poor and troubled. He started out as a broke janitor, then saved a week's worth of his pay and the way he spent it changed his life. Robbins was the oldest of three siblings and his mother was addicted to drugs and alcohol and was physically abusive. Out of necessity to protect his siblings, he became a virtual psychologist. He has stated that he attended schools where he was seen by other students as being from the wrong side of the tracks and by the time he was a junior in high school, he became fixated on the question of what separated the 'haves' from the 'have nots'? The popular kids from the outcasts.

At seventeen he worked as a janitor after school and helped people move on the weekends to make money to help out his family. It was on one of these moves, that he asked the landlord why he was a success, after Robbin's father had told him he was such a loser. The man told him that he started to turn his life around after going to a Jim Rohn seminar, which he described as 'a man who takes everything he's learned in twenty-thirty years of his life and he pours it into four hours.' Robbins asked him if he could get in for free, but the landlord refused because he knew he wouldn't value it. Tony then decided to save the thirty-five dollars needed to buy a ticket to the upcoming seminar out of his weekly wage of forty dollars and that's where things started to change for him.

Tony Robbins, who is now valued in the billions of dollars, knows the value behind finding deeper meaning and purpose in life. He became very clear he wanted to use and apply what he learned not only through Jim Rohn, but his own life experiences to help others. He is now arguably one of the world's leading authority in coaching people to personal and professional success. He learned the value of developing an inner self-confidence by re-examining his map of the world, his core values and beliefs and still leads the way in proactivity.

Tony Robbins is just an ordinary person like you and me and the reason I included him in this book is to inspire you. If a young, underprivileged kid with a mother addicted to drugs and alcohol, with very little to no resources to help him change his life can do it, so can you. A great starting point to finding out exactly what it is you want to do in life is to develop a purpose statement. Without a clear purpose statement, everything we do in life can become meaningless and unfulfilling and can create inner conflict. Our purpose statement needs to reflect the values that are important to us, so the actions we do daily become directed, meaningful and targeted. If the actions we do take don't feel right, it's because they're in collision with one or more core values and/or beliefs. Often people don't realise what this uneasiness is from, but it's important to understand why you feel that. Physiologically, this uneasiness can feel like your stomach is churning or your heart is beating faster. You may even feel nauseated. It's this inner conflict that will cause a person to act out, which creates inconsistent results, because they do not have a clear sense of direction. Without a clear sense of direction, a person is just going through the motions of life and not creating sustaining and long-lasting success, that creates a sense of inner peace.

Wouldn't it be great to wake up in the morning and jump out of bed and look forward to the day and going to work? That's how it should be. But for so many who have lost their way and become another average Joe trying to make ends meet to pay the rent and put food on the table, this is how life looks to them – dull, unexciting and even dreading Monday mornings. Life is not meant to be this way and the good news is that it doesn't have to stay that way. It's by taking stock of things and realising there's an issue within that exciting change can occur. The first step in creating meaningful change is developing a purpose statement.

When it comes to purpose statements, not a lot of people have thought about setting aside time to create one which fascinates me. We spend time planning holidays, planning the destination of our next vacation and going over all the finer details to make sure everything is as we want it to be. Why is it then, we don't dedicate that kind of time to planning our lives? Without clarity we cannot reap the benefits of satisfaction and joy because we aren't willing to put in the time to find out what it is we want to do in life. We aren't willing to set aside the time to plan and prepare and instead dream up all sorts of reasons and excuses as to why things are the way they are and things can't change.

Therefore, we stay stuck. We get stuck in meaningless jobs, meaningless relationships and wonder why we aren't happy. Creating a purpose statement would help rectify this and give a better sense of what direction we want to take in life and what's important to us. It creates clarity and guidance for meaningful action. Without self-assessing things won't change. Using the excuse that things can't change is choosing *not* to and that's just not good enough. We need to stop telling ourselves stories to justify being stuck and stagnant and get on with really living. The only way to do that is to begin.

When beginning to look at a purpose statement it's important to recognise what drives you. Are you principle and value centred and driven to make a difference in your own and other people's lives or are you success-driven and want to make a tonne of money no matter what the cost? These are just examples of course, but it is critical to become aware of these inner drives, as the ultimate driver is value-driven and principle centred where authenticity, integrity, responsibility and accountability lie. With these types of qualities, you will be the type of person who will be sought after to do business with and other like-minded people will naturally be drawn to you. Your circle of influence will be of the highest quality, because you took the time to re-evaluate, to re-design your map of the world, evaluate your core values and beliefs and align them with your purpose statement. As a result, new and healthier habits are formed with action and meaning in them. With all of this work it is important to honour your natural talents and align your purpose statement with these inner qualities, so that uneasiness from within ceases to exist and a new you can begin to shine.

A success-driven person whose primary motive is to make money and win at all costs, will not be the type of person who will be happy in the long run. Granted, they may have made a lot of money in their chosen career, but *how* they've accomplished success at the expense of others is not the type of person who you want to be emulating. They're not the ideal type of person to model. Their mindset is not a win-win; it is a win-lose. Meaning and purpose for people like this has a dollar sign attached to it. It will always cost you more than it costs them.

People who are driven by money and success are the type of people who exude characteristics like arrogance, domination, aggressive/passive behaviour and are those whose self-esteem is unstable. They feed off those around them, dominating to make themselves feel whole at the expense of others. These are the type of people when things go wrong, won't take ownership and responsibility for their part, but will blame external or outside influences for their own mistakes. They're the type of people you won't be able to count on in times of need, as they will seek to protect themselves first without a second thought for anyone else.

A simple example is if they were late to work one day, they would come up with reasons why it was external factors that caused them to be late. It was because the traffic was bad, the alarm didn't go off or the car wouldn't start. A more serious example would be blaming you for their mistakes, which can have disastrous consequences for you if you were their work colleague. This driver, the success at all costs type, is not one I recommend, but the values and principle centred driving force is the ideal model to use instead. It's founded on integrity and is far more respected by others. The foundations for this driver are set in a clear purpose statement.

A personal mission statement creates boundaries and gives guidance and meaning. Everything you do with your time, money and relationships should fit within the boundaries of that mission statement to align with your core values and beliefs, as the results you seek are purpose-driven and meaningful. Boundaries within your mission statement are necessary, as this avoids procrastinating and meaningless activities and allows you to focus on the things that matter and are important. It's interesting that creating boundaries actually will free you up, because we naturally think of boundaries as restrictions, but in this case, they are the guiding principles that help you use time effectively and meaningfully.

To give you a couple of examples of purpose statements, so you can see where I am heading with this, my purpose statement is the following:

"I Aisha Alim know that my purpose in life is to lead, teach, guide and inspire others to be the best they can be and be an example of love and light. I always give my best, I have high expectations of myself and others, am principle centred and empathetic and love to learn and grow. I will always laugh and mix things up through my dynamic personality."

My purpose (or mission) statement took me quite a bit of time to come up with and I fiddled with it until I was happy with the statement reflecting what I am all about. For me, the qualities of leading, teaching, guiding and inspiring others helps direct the type of activities I engage in and in particular, the work I do. It is very important to me that I not only live congruently with my values like wisdom and love, but that every action I take helps propel myself and others forward. I aim to better the lives of others, I like to lead by example and so my mission statement needs to reflect my natural drivers in life. It is quite a simple one, but it is the one that works for me.

Some other examples of purpose statements I came across have designed theirs a little differently. The important thing is that it reflects the individual who wrote it and it guides their daily actions and activities they participate in. Purpose statements do not include meaningless activities that don't stimulate a person's creativity or allow their heart to sing. Quite the opposite in fact. Each statement has taken time to design, has more than likely had a few edits and additions along the way, until they've come up with a statement that work for them.

The first example is a generalised personal mission statement. Remember there's no right or wrong with this activity, the idea is that it needs to work for you. If any of the examples help you design your statement, then feel free to use some of the sentences for yourself – but only if they really speak to you.

"To constantly be striving to be the best version of myself – in my job, with my health and fitness, with my relationships with family and friends and with my emotional well-being."

"My mission in life is not merely to survive, but to thrive; and to do so with some passion, some compassion, some humour and some style."

"I think the most important part of my life is my family and my close friends. I would love to soon start my own family and fulfil my professional dream of owning my accounting firm. Both family and business require attention and love. I value hard work, honesty and responsibility in my personal and professional lives."

In Stephen Covey's book, *The Seven Habits of Highly Effective People*, he has provided two other examples of mission statements which are different again and worthy of including. Covey's friend Rolfe Kerr, has expressed his personal creed in the following way.

"Succeed at home first.

Seek and merit divine help.

Never compromise with honesty.

Remember the people involved.

Hear both sides before judging.

Obtain counsel of others.

Defend those who are absent.

Be sincere yet decisive.

Develop one new proficiency a year.

Plan tomorrow's work today.

Hustle while you wait.

Maintain a positive attitude.

Keep a sense of humour.

Be orderly in person and in work.

Do not fear mistakes – fear only the absence of creative, constructive and corrective responses to those mistakes.

Facilitate the success of subordinates.

Listen twice as much as you speak.

Concentrate all abilities and efforts on the task at hand, not worrying about the next job or promotion."

Finally, a woman seeking to balance family and work values has expressed her personal mission a little differently.

"I will seek to balance career and family as best I can since both are important to me. My home will be a place where I and my family, friends and guests find joy, comfort, peace and happiness. Still, I will seek to create a clean and orderly environment, yet liveable and comfortable. I will exercise wisdom in what we choose to eat, read, see and do at home. I especially want to teach my children to love, to learn and to laugh – and to work and develop their unique talents.

I value the rights, freedoms and responsibilities of our democratic society. I will be a concerned and informed citizen, involved in the political process to ensure my voice is heard and my vote is counted. I will be a self-starting individual who exercises initiative in accomplishing my life's goals. I will act on situations and opportunities, rather than to be acted upon.

I will always try to keep myself free from addictive and destructive habits. I will develop habits that free me from old labels and limits and expand my capabilities and choices.

My money will be my servant, not my master. I will seek financial independence over time. My wants will be subject to my needs and my means. Except for long-term home and car loans, I will seek to keep myself free from consumer debt. I will spend less than I earn and regularly save or invest part of my income.

Moreover, I will use what money and talents I have to make life more enjoyable for others through service and charitable giving."

As the examples indicate, they have set clear boundaries of what they will or won't accept in their lives and each gives clarity, meaning and purpose for their goals both personally and professionally. If something comes up that is outside of these boundaries, they don't have to worry about deciding on whether to act on it, because the decision has been made already – it's that simple. If it is written in your mission statement or in line with it – then do it. If it isn't, then don't.

People spend so much time deciding whether they're going to do something or not. People that is that haven't written a purpose statement. Should I do it? What if I don't do it? I could be doing…These cause people unnecessary stress and are a classic time-wasting activity. A mission statement acts as a guide, a blueprint if you like to help you on a day to day basis, so your life and the directions you take become easier and more straightforward. It encompasses your values and what you believe to be true about yourself and where you're heading in life and can be a tremendous reference point as well.

My suggestion is that when you have come up with one that suits you, put it up on your wall, design it how you like but keep it in full view. Some of my clients who have done this activity, decided to put a daily reminder on their phone with a summary of their statement, to remind them throughout the day what their purpose statement encompassed. It served as a reminder as to what was important and took priority each day with the benefit of building confidence through meaningful action. How you choose to do your own purpose or mission statement is up to you and as I said, feel free to use any of the examples I gave to help kick start your own.

I'd also suggest that you do this in your quiet, uninterrupted moments of the day in a place where you won't be disturbed. It takes time to self-reflect and evaluate your needs and wants and hopefully, you've already identified your core values from the exercise I gave on values at the start of the book. Use those values and align them with what's most important to you to start the ball rolling. As I said, my own statement took some time to finally get right and a lot of cross outs and re-writes, but a purpose statement isn't something you can just pull out of thin air. There are however, questions you can begin asking yourself that will move you closer to creating one.

1. What is important? Identify what or whom you value and how your life is connected to those things.

2. Where do I want to go? You can answer this in many different ways – it

is different for everybody. Your answer may involve a spiritual, mental or physical destination or encompass your career objectives and/or family ones. Like the examples, it is entirely different for each person and remember there are no right or wrong answers.

3. What does 'the best' look like for me? Describe your ultimate outcome or results you want for yourself. This isn't about being realistic; it is about your dreams.

4. How do I want to act? How do you want people to describe you? What qualities do you want to demonstrate daily? List some words or phrases you would love people to use when they think about you.

5. What kind of legacy do you want to leave behind? How would you like to be remembered? What type of impact have you left on other people's lives? It can be simple and sweet or as complex and high impact as you like. Just remember, this is your legacy and no-one else's.

Some coaches will advise you to keep your mission statement to a minimum of one or two sentences at most. This is primarily because you want to be able to remember it so it naturally rolls off the tongue. Initially, when you begin a purpose statement, like in the example I gave about the mother, it may be quite long. In that case, ideally it should be displayed so that others who are affected by it can also see what the mission or goals are. It can serve as a daily reminder for others as well. However, don't get caught up in the semantics of conforming to what other people do. If your statement is longer or shorter than the examples I gave it makes no difference. If you have key words written up as well – awesome! The important thing is that it works for you.

When designing your purpose statement don't forget about others as well. Yes, it is a personal mission statement, but it should be just as much about the people you want to impact as it is about yourself. Make sure it reflects that too, as this encompasses the point about leaving a legacy. It could be as simple as teaching another person how to build something or teaching your child how to manage money for the future. Whatever it is, it needs to include this element.

Once you've started designing it, you may want to get some input from those that matter in your life such as family members, work colleagues or influential role models that you admire. It's helpful to get some feedback and they can also provide you with invaluable insight as well. This will allow you to make adjustments to it. Just remember it's not set in stone and will change as you grow and learn – that's natural. As long as you're staying true to the mission you know you were put here to accomplish you can't go wrong.

To help you further with some of the wording challenges you may face I found a few more purpose statements to assist you. These are designed to inspire you so use any of the words from these examples or those I previously mentioned.

"To inspire positive change through teaching and coaching."

"To encourage everyone I interact with on a daily basis."

"To create opportunities for today's youth."

"To help others live the lives they would if they only knew how."

"My personal career mission is to become a world-class aeronautical engineer in the commercial aviation industry."

"It is my mission to live a life of honesty, integrity and unconditional love and carry those qualities to every aspect of my life. I will hold myself accountable and live by my values and beliefs."

As I mentioned earlier, there will be times when an activity or task is put in front of you which will cause a sense of uneasiness for you. Trust that instinct and remember your purpose statement. The decision whether to participate or not, has been made easy for you by design and all you have to do is stay true to yourself and your integrity and it becomes easy. It takes time and practice and you are bound to make mistakes. The key is not to fall into the trap of feeling sorry for yourself again and blaming circumstances or others for your own quality of life. It's time for accountability and purposeful action. This is where you need to aim to be in life. Holding yourself accountable to your purpose statement and not continuing to be distracted or irresponsible anymore. Aligning your daily actions with your purpose in life creates an inner excitement and zest for life. Hiccups along the way will happen, but it's how you handle them when things don't go according to plan, that reflects your level of maturity and growth.

Everyone has issues, everyone has problems they need to deal with, but the difference between success and failure is how you deal with setbacks and rejection. Are you the type of person who sits back feeling sorry for themselves remarking 'it isn't fair' or are you the type of person who learns from a negative experience, takes it on the chin and just gets on with it? You may not be quite there yet and that's okay, but the key is having a willingness to learn and an open mind for change. Having a willingness to accept new understandings to apply in your own life, allows transformation to occur. It won't happen overnight but it will happen. It takes time for you to evolve into the person you were born to be. It takes time to undo the indented maps you formed and to let go of labels that have held you back. I guarantee if you put the work in and you have a determined and willing spirit it will happen. You will live the life you were born to live. You just have to commit to the process one hundred percent and it starts today.

Tool 5

=—c

Letting go of the past

"You have to make the decision to let go of the past if you want to move forward. Reliving your painful past will poison your heart and your tomorrow. If you look at today through the eyes of the past, you can never see what the present moment has to offer."
Bryant McGill

Part of creating a new future for ourselves is the ability to let go of the past. The past has often been the thing that trips up so many and has also been a source of weaponry for others to use against us, particularly from family and/or close friends. Sometimes it can spur individuals onto succeed, but the past can also be used against us time and time again – if we allow it to. However, the past is the past and looking back only serves to keep us stuck and trapped there.

Every person has events in their past that they're not proud of no matter how big or small they are, but it doesn't help when those closest to you continually remind you of those errors. By knowing ourselves well, by being confident enough within ourselves to assertively stand our ground, we can start moving forward in life. But how do we move forward when others are constantly reminding us of sins of the past? The best way to combat that is to live a life of purpose and meaning. It will silence the critics!

There are issues that a person must deal with and they'll be different for everyone, but it takes time, patience and self-reflection to learn from those errors and cease old behavioural patterns and start learning new ones. Counselling has its place especially for issues of a serious nature, but the important thing is once the issue has been thoroughly addressed and the individual feels confident enough to move forward, it's time to learn new ways of acting and reacting and new ways of behaving and thinking. It is a time to get excited about the future. The door to new opportunities is opening. Being open to change and learning how to be free from the grip of anxiety and fear and cease those old patterns of behaviour, is the next step to be taking.

I deliberately used the word excited as the feelings of anxiousness and excitement are the same physiological response within the body. It's the associated images and attachments we create around those internal feelings that determine how we perceive things. For example, if I went to the fair with my friend and she wanted me to go on the rollercoaster with her, she could perceive the ride as an adrenalin rush full of excitement, whereas, I may see it as terrifying. I still have the same adrenalin rush as she does, but I've associated fear with the ride and she hasn't. How I perceive the ride as opposed to my friend is different. I'm scared, she's not. It's the associations we've both created around the ride that's determined our response to it. The associated feelings and thoughts then determine what actions we take as a result. She would more than likely go on the ride, whereas I would be the bystander watching on.

How we perceive new opportunities will determine the type of experience we get. Seeing new situations as an opportunity to learn, to better oneself and a chance to excel is being proactive and positive. We are beginning to unlearn some of the old habits of being problem focused and shifting our mindset to being open and no longer closed off. I must add here that there is a fine line between talking issues through to the stage of acceptance and talking them through to where it becomes the sole topic of conversation. If a person isn't aware enough it can become linked to their identity.

Some people who are still in that phase of talking about an event in their past, even when the trauma and shock have diminished, can stay stuck there. Even when the event has happened years ago, the lingering effects, the tattered self-confidence and painful experiences seem to remain at the forefront of their mind. Learning to let go of the events, learning to love yourself enough to want more for yourself and learning to forgive, are critical steps to take in moving forward. Letting go of the past can be hard work, but I guarantee, the harder you have to work at doing it, the more rewarding it feels once you've come through the other side.

It's almost like a sense of victory; you've climbed that treacherous mountain and you've succeeded, planting your flag proudly on the mountain peak. It's important not to forget how far you've come, how hard you worked and all the trips and tumbles you took to get there. You can now plant a new memory at the forefront of your mind – a positive, empowering memory, that uses the event from the past and how you used your strength to conquer it. You built a tower of resilience by doing so and best of all, the person who reaps the rewards for all that work is you. You've climbed that mountain and built the foundations using strength and courage.

A way to think about it is, how do you want to be remembered? What legacy do you want to leave and what example are you setting? Do you want to be remembered as someone who always talked about past events, about being a victim, or do you want to be remembered as an incredible example of self-determination, of wanting more and striving to get it? It seems an obvious choice but often our actions and our self-talk does not reflect these changes and we keep looking backwards, in danger of becoming complacent with ourselves and staying comfortable. Even though it may be a little difficult to hear, the sympathy and the validation of how bad things were for you and the conversations you've now become accustomed to, can be hard to let go of. It's also a way of telling yourself you're justified in acting the way you do and thinking and feeling that way as well. That's the trap right there. The excuses we tell ourselves for why we are the way we are, become the trap we fall victim to.

It's our past's fault, it's our parents fault, it's the home environment I grew up in's fault and on it goes. It's a way of feeling somehow justified from an event from the past where you may have felt powerless and/or guilty, for not living up to your potential now. It's almost like you're entitled to feel the way you do, that it is somehow your right. The issue is it isn't healthy to constantly blame others or circumstances for the way things have turned out for you. It doesn't justify or give you a reason for not experiencing satisfaction and happiness in your life as an adult. Others aren't responsible for the level of happiness you experience in life – only you are, no matter how many times you tell yourself otherwise. At some point, we need to realise that as grown adults we can't keep blaming our past for how things are for us now. We need to grow the heck up and start taking responsibility for ourselves and the level of happiness we want to experience. It's time to stop whinging, it's time to stop the traps of self-pity and get on with it.

Children who grow up within domestic violent homes for example, can turn into adults with huge baggage from the past that has the potential to ruin relationships with others in the future. As children, their vulnerability, their very essence, has been rocked to the core and without becoming aware of repetitive self-sabotaging behaviours and negative self-talk, positive growth and development will evade them.

A huge hurdle for people who've experienced such things is forgiveness of self. Letting go of the guilt of not being able to help, of not being able to stop the violence and that feeling of helplessness, can transpose itself into huge amounts of guilt into adulthood – if we allow it to. Forgiving ourselves is a crucial step, because we didn't know then what we know now. It's important to remember that when we look back to how things were then, we are doing so with the lenses of hindsight, which is now subject to more knowledge and power. Being gentle and kind with ourselves in this step is a must.

The maps we've grown up with, the ingrained views formed due to the experiences we've had, then form the basis of our expectations for future relationships. Because that vulnerability as children was exploited, abused or neglected, the adult (female) version of these children, will tend to engage in attention-seeking behaviours to feel loved, worthy, validated and secure. They are yet to experience love and security that is principle centred and founded on strong family values. Because it was given in a way that was not unconditional (if at all), they tend to go looking for that love and sense of security in all the wrong ways.

Those feelings of insecurity can manifest themselves in behaviours such as wearing heavy makeup to feel attractive and desirable and deliberately seeking the approval of men to validate their low levels of self-worth. It can take the form of being overly loud, compensating for the past, when as children they were told to be quiet or that their opinion on things didn't matter or count. They seek the approval of others, wanting people to notice them and can even act out against the rules of home and/or society, forming addictive tendencies and sexual promiscuity can result as well.

I'm not saying that all of these things will occur, but many of them can happen if the person doesn't realise they are spiralling out of control. That need for security, love and for feeling safe and validated for who they are, begin being met in ways they've seen or experienced growing up or overcompensating for what they didn't get. The wearing of heavy makeup can be a feeling of power and control and for wanting their beauty validated. Because they were powerless growing up and experienced some type of trauma when they were vulnerable, the makeup can be a safeguard that acts as a shield to prevent their innocence from being violated again. Their inner beauty was stifled and never given a chance to shine. By wearing makeup, they give their inner-self a voice of its own, projecting an air of confidence that doesn't wholly exist intrinsically. They seek validation externally, satisfying the need by receiving flattering remarks which justifies the makeup being a necessity, to hold up the already flimsy levels of self-worth. Their confidence relies on external measurements and so it creates a cycle of addictive behaviours to keep that mask of confidence up.

Because as children they may have observed women being validated by men for looking beautiful, it has created a subconscious map whereby 'if I look good, things will be good'. Because their confidence levels are shaky, getting that validation from men has created the wrong type of mindset. She feels that she is only worthy of love if she looks desirable, but she's being desired in the wrong ways. There's a mismatch of intentions which creates even more confusion for her and the cycle of having to mask her pain continues by shielding it with makeup. She hasn't learned how to be desired in the right ways yet. She hasn't experienced what is like to be loved for who she truly is.

Being desired for being a giving and thoughtful person, being desired for the way you nurture and care for children or for having an amazing personality and being outgoing and funny. Of course as women we want to feel we are beautiful, but it's not the only thing we want to feel attractive for. There are plenty of examples I could use, but my point is, the wearing of heavy makeup is sometimes an indication of a person's level of confidence, if they're needing it to feel good about themselves and to be validated by the opposite sex. The interesting thing is, if you speak to men about the whole makeup topic, most men will tell you that they are attracted to women who wear little to no makeup, preferring them to look natural. They are attracted to confident, self-assured women, who don't seek or need the approval of others to feel good about themselves. This is a highly attractive quality in women that men are drawn to, as men like to feel wanted and not needed to boost the confidence levels of females. It's taxing and tiring, so scaling back the amount of makeup women use does have its benefits for both.

The acting out and anti-social behaviour can go hand in hand and so can sexual promiscuity. Going out, seeking the perfect man, the perfect partner (not like the role model you had growing up) takes commitment. Not knowing how to attract the right type of man or having the skills or understanding necessary to find Mr Right, nightclubs and drinking alcohol become the weekend thing in the hope that you'll meet him, fall in love and live happily ever after. And of course, all of that will start in a nightclub, right? Wrong!

Although it can't be seen at the time, the nightclub scene is in essence, like a meat market for men and women to scour the room to seek out a potential mate for the night. For those who are wanting more, wanting a long-term commitment, the intention is completely different. However, the fact remains that one night stands and brief sexual interludes will lead a person to feeling used and even more unworthy of what they desire – true love. It's like a vicious cycle; trying to express unconditional love in a very intimate way but not realising it's the wrong way to get it. The sad truth is, for some women they get almost addicted to this type of behaviour, because even though the night with their chosen male companion was brief, for those moments they felt loved, desired and accepted. It's when the moment ends their world comes crashing down and once again they feel unworthy of love. The pattern of behaviour continues to be cyclic; the more she tries to find love, the more she repeats old patterns of behaviour leading her to self-loathe if she isn't careful. The sad fact is a woman in this situation hasn't learned to love herself enough to know she is worthy of more – yet.

Another self-destructive behaviour that can result from traumatised backgrounds, is the need for substances such as alcohol and drugs to numb the pain of the past. This band aid effect of covering the pain and not wanting to take responsibility for one's actions (or inability to act), shows a lack of maturity and learned skills. Living in denial is easier. The effects of these substances not only harm physically and psychologically, but they affect a person's emotional wellbeing and their level of self-worth as well. Unless the person who is in the situation can recognise they're on a path of self-destruction, nothing will change. The band aid needs to be taken off permanently and replaced instead with new learnings and understandings that will aid a person's aspirations in life. It's when we recognise we are worthy of more, worthy of being loved, worthy of a truly satisfying and happy life, that we will chase *that* instead and not the endless, temporary fix that the alcohol or drugs give.

As a result of these experiences, of being in a toxic environment where formed patterns of behaviour have become the norm, it can be difficult to accept that you played a major part in it as well. Forgiveness is a huge part of letting go of the past and can be one of the most challenging to accomplish. Forgiveness of self is hard and can cause many trips and tumbles on the way up to the top of that mountain. It's during those times when we do struggle, that the resultant outcome of triumph becomes even more valuable to us.

Being able to examine the event/s of the past and being able to acknowledge your part in it is a huge step forward. As children we are powerless to do anything about the situation at the time and learning to forgive yourself is critical. Guilt and shame can cloud a person for years and serves no purpose at all. It can become an excuse for being stuck in the trap of self-pity or self-righteousness, where we can think we're entitled to feel the way we do. As adults who've survived domestic violence, it's now time to take responsibility for ourselves and our actions – it's time to grow up. It's time to embrace our own power and create an amazing future that is not bound by events from the past. It's time to break free of the shackles that once chained us down and step into our own uniqueness.

That negative self-talk is one of the hardest to let go of and I'm not implying that you will hang onto it deliberately, not at all. Because the things we tell ourselves are repetitive and become a pattern of behaviour, it's easy to not even realise that's what we are doing. Until we become aware of the negative self-talk and the destructiveness of it, nothing will change. Once you realise that the world you are creating for yourself is all within you, things can change. When you have the epiphany that the way you have been living your life hasn't been serving you, that the years of repetitive behavioural patterns you've become accustomed to haven't been productive and you're worthy of more, things will begin to change.

Being able to let go of the past and the pain and anguish associated with past events is a leap forward. Forgiving yourself and others for what happened is a major breakthrough to achieve. It's like the ball and chain analogy; once you cut the chain loose, the heaviness of that ball (the past) is lightened. The chains have been cut, freeing you to spend time in other pursuits. But give time, time. Be patient with the process and be especially kind to yourself. With time and plenty of repetitive practice things will change, but it will only happen when you're completely committed to it.

Quite often people struggle with the concept of forgiveness and why it plays such a critical role in propelling a person forward. As someone who has worked through this myself and struggled at first to understand this concept, my advice is to remember that the forgiveness stage is for you and not for them. When I talk about forgiving someone for past actions, I'm talking about forgiving the pain and heartache it caused you so that you can be set free from it. I'm not talking about forgiving the act itself and making that distinction is important. We need to understand the difference between the actions and the pain the event caused. You can't control another person's actions or the way they feel only your own and so forgiveness in this sense serves to help you and you alone. Choosing to forgive sets you free from the burden of carrying that pain around with you. It gives you power and control and puts you in the driver's seat to move forward in life. One way of doing this is being able to analyse the situation and use terms like: 'I forgive the pain and heartache he/she caused me so that I can be free from it.' 'I choose to forgive ___ so that I am not bound by the past anymore.' 'I am letting go of the pain, anger and frustration I feel in order to move forward in my life.'

These statements are examples only and you need to find what works best for you and your situation. It's such an important step in change, it is freeing to go through this stage and look back with a sense of pride, knowing that you've overcome a major hurdle in helping you move forward. One thing I will say is, don't expect change to occur instantaneously because it won't. Some people do it alone, some people work with professionals – it's entirely up to you. You need to practice it and be patient with yourself during this process and when the negative self-talk creeps back in, turn away from it and remind yourself how far you've come and how worthwhile this stage is. It'll inevitably happen, as old patterns don't go that easily, but the more you do it the stronger you become and the weaker the negativity gets. You're climbing that mountain with determination and grit. There will be a few trips and tumbles along the way but by golly you're climbing it! What a mountain you've climbed and the power and control are now all with you.

I'd like to finish this chapter with a true story about the power of forgiveness and letting go of the past. One of the women who participated in my women's empowerment course in 2020, applied what she had learned in class quite literally. She shared in class what transpired as a result of her applying this tool and by her permission, am including an excerpt of what she shared with us that day. This is Emma's story and the power this tool really has.

"Through Aisha's teachings and her speaking about letting go of the pain of the past and how holding onto hate will inhibit and consume you, it got me thinking about my own past. She told us how holding onto that pain causes you to be consumed by hate and that we will never find peace that way. I listened as she explained to us that we aren't condoning their actions, but we are letting go of the pain those actions caused us, so we can be free of all the unjust guilt we carry around. I wanted that.

The night of February 8th, 2008, my brother was brutally murdered by two men at the front of the primary school. He was 18 years old. My brother was in the wrong place at the wrong time and the two men gave no reason why they killed him. One of the men pleaded guilty, whilst the other put my family and I through an unnecessary drawn out murder trial. The man who pleaded guilty showed genuine remorse and received 20 years' jail with 16 years for good behaviour, the other received 23 years' jail.

Through what Aisha taught us, it got me thinking about the man who pleaded guilty and his family and the pain and heartache they must have felt too. I had been consumed with my own pain and anger and never stopped to think about how they would have felt. They hadn't done anything wrong and yet their lives were changed forever too. I decided to reach out to the family and his sister was the first to contact me and then his Mum.

Through our correspondence, I wanted them to know that I didn't hate or blame them and that just like me, they too, had been carrying around unjust guilt as well.

I hadn't stopped to consider anyone else's pain at the time, as I had been consumed by my own. As a result of our correspondence, they felt a sense of relief and I decided to take one more step to close the door on the pain of the past and its grip on me. I decided to write to the man who killed my brother in jail. The man who showed remorse that is.

I ended up writing to him, telling him how I forgave him and that I will never condone the act, but that I forgave him and have no hatred towards him. I went on to say that past mistakes do not define a person, it's how they pick themselves up and move forward that does. The only way he could show true remorse is upon his release, he lives the best possible version of himself he can and he does it for both himself and my brother's memory. Then his death wouldn't be in vain. His family were so very grateful, I was not expecting this overall sense of lightness, like a heavy weight had been lifted from all of us. The unexpected thing was, he wrote back to me, thanking me and promising me to live the best possible life he could and he was very gracious and sincere in what he wrote. I felt so incredibly powerful and free. It's hard to explain just how much I felt.

None of this would have occurred without Aisha's guidance. It was through her teachings, I was not only able to give myself closure, but I was able to give so many other people closure too. I still think about my brother every day and the reality of the pain and fear he felt in his final moments, but I'm not bound by the past anymore. I know my brother would have been proud of what I have done."

Tool 6

Stopping negative self-talk

"You've been criticising yourself for years and it hasn't worked. Try approving of yourself and see what happens."

Louise Hay

"Whatever you hold in your mind on a consistent basis is exactly what you will experience in your life."

Tony Robbins

Negative self-talk, what we tell ourselves is arguably the hardest thing to change of all. Letting go of the past, forgiving ourselves and others, helps us on our journey, because we are also letting go of any bitterness and anger we may be holding onto. If we are holding onto bitterness and anger it consumes us, which then transpires into some degree of negative self-talk. A question to ask yourself is, if I hold onto the bitterness, hatred or anger I feel is it going to help me in the future? If within your mind you instantly said no, then this process is definitely for you. Part of change is recognising what we are holding onto, what we are justifying and what we're telling ourselves. Becoming aware of self-talk, our conversations with others, how we behave and how we feel is a major leap forward in self-transformation. The hardest habit of all to change is negative self-talk – what we tell ourselves.

Letting go of negative self-talk is a challenge but it's a challenge only you can decide to take on. Personal power is making empowered decisions with positive actions. Changing ingrained patterns of destructive, self-sabotaging behaviours, means changing the negative self-talk. Changing negative self-talk naturally changes a person's outward behaviours leading to a more empowered and satisfying life.

Most people would be able to relate well to the inner-critic – the inner voice that judges and doubts you and seems to belittle you. It is full of negativity and criticism and seems to constantly remind you that you're not worthy or good enough of anything better. It says negative, hurtful things to you, things you'd never say to another human being and yet we say these things to ourselves. How is that okay? Phrases like, 'I am such an idiot.' 'I'm a failure.' 'I'm hopeless at everything I do.' 'I never do anything right.' 'I'll never succeed at anything'. As these phrases indicate, we tend to make sweeping generalised negative statements when something goes wrong, applying it across all other aspects of our lives. When we do this, we start believing those to be true and it creates a reality that is negative by nature and self-defeating. It becomes a vicious cycle.

For example, we may not experience success with landing our dream job the first, second or even third time around because we may not have interviewed well. Let's assume the reason is a lack of preparedness for the interview. Instead of looking at the interview as a reference point to learn and improve on, we tend to jump to the conclusion that we aren't any good and start telling ourselves we're hopeless and can't succeed. Just because one or two interviews didn't go too well, doesn't translate into 'I'm no good at anything and I'll never be successful'. It's not a reason to fail or an excuse to quit trying. If we aren't careful, we smudge that negative judgement and all of a sudden we believe we're a failure in everything we do in life. We're on the self-pity cycle of negative self-talk once more.

Like it or not everything you say to yourself does matter. The inner critic is harmful and it only serves to inhibit, limit and stop you from pursuing the life you truly want to live. If a person, like in the example of the job interview, allowed the negative self-talk to take over, allowed the inner critic to dominate their thoughts, they would more than likely end up developing an irrational fear of failure and may even stop applying for further work. That one interview that didn't go well, has now been the entrée the inner critic needed to serve up a main course of criticism, judgement and a sweeping generalisation of hopelessness. If left unchecked, if a person doesn't become aware and take control, it can lead to serious mental health issues such as anxiety and/or depression.

Choosing the inner critic, choosing to talk negatively to yourself, is exactly that – a choice. Building awareness gives you power and control over it. We don't often realise that it actually is a choice and if left unchecked, it can lead us to feeling disempowered. Having said that, the inner critic does have a purpose, as long as the self-talk you're telling yourself is positive. It's like choosing to be punished over being rewarded which seems an obvious choice. It's only human nature to want to be rewarded for what we do. It is not human nature to want to be punished. Why is it then that we allow our mind to wander blindly without taking control of our conscious thoughts? Without awareness and becoming attuned to our inner thoughts, that negative self-talk continues to rule and dominate. It needs to be kept in check.

To explain my point a little further, think of a young person who has committed a miserly crime of stealing a packet of lollies and is punished by imprisonment. Besides the outrage of being imprisoned, the amount of damage that punishment would do psychologically would be immense. However, if the young person had explained to them the value of not stealing, of the consequences for the shop owner, for themselves and the effect it could have on their future, wouldn't that be better than the severity of the punishment? Wouldn't choosing to re-educate, to explain and advise the possible effects of doing such an act be a better choice to make? Whilst punishment can deter certain behaviours in the short-term, rewards (or in this case re-education), are generally better for shaping new and lasting behaviours. Why then do we choose to punish ourselves, choose not to re-educate and choose not to reward our steps towards positive change? With negative self-talk, that's exactly what we're doing.

When you punish someone for what they do wrong that doesn't teach them how to do it right. Imagine a small child learning to walk. If you scream at him, call him stupid or dumb every time he falls, can you imagine the damage that negative talk would have on his future development? However, if every time he fell you smiled and helped him up, encouraged him to keep learning, that would have a very different effect indeed – a positive and healthy one. When the inner critic consistently negatively labels, it has a demoralising effect and helps determine the level of self-worth a person has and their beliefs about their capabilities become capped. Whether or not the critic is right or not is irrelevant. Negative self-talk is never in your best interests and there are always different, kinder and better ways to treat yourself, that doesn't involve negative labels and a self-destructive mindset.

In any given situation you can choose to focus on what you did right or what you did wrong. If you didn't do well in a task, ask yourself why. Did I prepare as well as I could have for that interview? Was I presented as well as I could be? Did I do some practice runs before the interview? These type of analyses of a situation are healthy and productive because it helps you to learn and grow from that experience. By taking a positive approach from what could potentially be viewed as a negative experience, you silence the negative self-talk and become empowered instead. If at the end of the day you did all you could to prepare for the interview and you still didn't get it, accept that this particular job wasn't meant to be and move on. Dwelling on the fact you didn't get it, when you know you did all you could, does nothing to help your future needs. Let it go.

Negative self-talk can be like a runaway freight train that is out of control. If no-one's got their foot on the brake to pull the train up, the train will end up crashing and burning. The same applies to us. If we don't learn ways to stop and overpower negative self-talk, it too, will get out of control and make us crash and burn. Two of the greatest words I ever learned when I found myself on the train of negative self-talk was stop it. The effectiveness of saying stop it works and works well and I recommend saying it audibly and not just to yourself. The reason is the spoken word has more power and effect than those we say to ourselves. It's simple, easy, quick and costs you nothing.

The following four steps will help you silence the inner critic and help you become a more positive, optimistic person in the process.

1. Notice the critic

To gain mastery over the inner critic you need first to become aware of it. During every conscious moment we have an inner dialogue with ourselves. A lot of that is automatic and doesn't take any real conscious thought and it happens so quickly, that we barely notice it before we move on to the next thought. Making the conscious effort to slow down and pay more attention to your thoughts, will help you notice when the critic is present. Your emotional state is also a good indication of when that cycle of negative self-talk is happening, as your emotions will cue you to the presence of the critic. Negative emotions such as shame, self-doubt and guilt are almost always signs of the critic at work.

A good exercise to try for a week to help you become aware of the presence of the inner critic and the effects it's having on you, is to write in your journal when you notice yourself being self-critical. Every time you notice yourself being self-critical, write down a summary of the situation. What was the trigger to the negative self-talk? Was it that you were late to work one day, had a fight with a friend or that you decided to eat junk for lunch instead of the sandwich you packed? Next to the event write down the negative self-talk you told yourself as a result of the experience. For example, because you were late to work, did you make the assumption and generalisation that you're lazy? Maybe you've told yourself you're useless because you can't even be on time to work. Whatever it is you told yourself at that moment, write it down. The idea is twofold; firstly, you're becoming more aware of what you're telling yourself and secondly, what the triggers were. By doing this step, you're now becoming more consciously aware of what you think.

2. Separate the critic from your identity

The inner critic doesn't want you to notice it. It thrives best when it goes unnoticed and is allowed to go unchecked. Just like the freight train speeding down the track, it needs stopping. What we need to realise is, that we weren't born with the internal critic, we weren't born with this seemingly automated negative self-talk garbage. We learned it. We learned it via influences from our environment such as other people's criticism and their expectations and standards they place on us and from what we have learned through other influences like our family. Being immersed in and around negative language, poor communication styles and a general lack of integrity and responsibility, has unintentionally been filtered into our consciousness without us realising it. Their influences are so great, that they have become part of our psyche and have been deeply imbedded. Being able to separate this critic, this 'thing' that has invaded us and has become part of our identity is important.

Try giving the negative self-talk a name, an identity of its own so every time it rears its ugly head you know that it's just 'Mr Grumpypants' in action and not you. By giving it a name, you've now separated the inner critic from yourself and created a second identity which is separate to your own. It's not a part of you anymore. You're the one in control and by doing this step it loosens its power over you.

3. Talkback

I touched earlier on two powerful words I learned and suggest my clients use as well, which was 'stop it'. Audibly saying these two words so you can hear yourself say them gives them power. You're now in the position where the inner critic, Mr Grumpypants (or whatever you've named it), is a separate entity from yourself. By saying 'stop it' you're taking back control, putting your foot on the brake and regaining your power as a result. You've become aware of triggers, created more conscious awareness and have managed to detach the negativity from your own identity by creating a separate identity for it. Talking back to it, silencing the critic, gives you power and control. Now you need to replace him because you've created a new, empowered and strong space. Letting go of the critic and tossing it aside, gives you freedom back and the ability to replace it with a positive identity. Remember to do this step consistently, as it's easy to fall back into old patterns of behaviours and self-criticise again. Talking back to it, showing it who's boss by speaking those words gives you a sense of control again.

4. Replace the critic

The best way to defeat the critic is to have an even stronger ally on your side, which is your unique inner voice. Every person is born perfect and pure and recognising your uniqueness is a powerful tool. You need to start noticing the *good* things about yourself and write them into your journal and give *that* a voice instead of the critic. Journaling about how good you are at something, writing about all the things you love doing, your skills and talents, what makes you happy, becomes your new focus. The important thing is you're learning to replace the inner critic with a new, fresh and positive attitude, that is part of your identity and it came naturally to you. What you're doing in this stage, is tapping back into all that you were born with, all you were gifted with, until the negative inner critic came and spoiled things. Now you're able to realise that you have so much to offer, that there's a tremendous amount of good in you and link *that* with your identity instead.

To get you started, try listing key qualities about yourself. For example, I am kind, giving, caring and strong. It doesn't have to be exactly this format, but this is a great way to begin taking ownership of your uniqueness. It's easy to say things about ourselves like I am a mother, I am a teacher, I am a good person – all the surface aspects of ourselves, but it's much harder to give a voice to those deeper qualities, particularly when you aren't used to doing it. Practice doing it until you are.

We become very good at listing off all the things we aren't good at, however, the more you focus on all the positive qualities, traits and aspects about yourself, the less time you waste worrying or criticising yourself.

On top of that, you have now silenced the inner critic, separated it from your own identity, taken ownership of what you tell yourself and are ready to be in the driver's seat again. You've stopped the freight train from being out of control and put the brakes on. Don't expect perfection in silencing the critic, that's unrealistic and only setting yourself up for failure. Just be aware that the critic won't go quite that easily, but patience and persistence are the keys to defeating him. The more you do it, the more he is squashed and the more you grow your positive inner voice and uniqueness at the same time. Again, practice is the key to silencing him.

Letting go of the past, letting go of negativity is a huge leap forward in transforming your life. Forgiveness of self and others, learning new and better ways of thinking and behaving is an exciting step to take. You are well on your way climbing the mountain of empowerment, taking it step by step to plant your flag at the top with successful transformation. Don't forget at the top of the mountain will be *your* name proudly displayed. Keep focused on that goal and do your best not to get distracted with old patterns of thinking that send you off course. Keep reminding yourself of not only your uniqueness, but just how far you've come already. You've come way too far to turn back now and the top of that mountain should now seem attainable and not just a pipe-dream anymore.

Questions for you:

1. What type of self-talk do you engage in consistently? Do you need to adjust the way you speak to yourself?

2. What have you decided to name the inner critic? What is his role in your life now?

3. What are your inner qualities? List them all and start owning it!

Tool 7

Our needs and their influence

"One of the basic needs of every human being is the need to be loved, to have our wishes and feelings taken seriously, to be validated as people who matter."

Harold S. Kushner

According to world-renowned expert on human behaviour, Tony Robbins, human beings have six core needs that drive every person and every decision they make, whether that be in a resourceful or dysfunctional way. As we begin to understand these needs further and what drives the decisions we make and the actions we take, we can then start to examine whether those behaviours and actions we are exhibiting are healthy or not and make adjustments accordingly.

Each day we fulfil these needs constructively or in a destructive, disempowering way. Once we develop greater awareness around these needs and why we do what we do, we can then consider other ways to meet these needs in a more resourceful way and create inner peace and harmony with our lives.

Depending on which of the six basic human needs are foremost in your personality, you could be spending a lot of time consciously or subconsciously trying to meet one or two of them. And if you don't succeed, it could negatively impact your overall sense of wellbeing. Knowing which of your six needs is your primary motivator and how this affects your ability to connect with others and develop healthy relationships, is crucial to your understanding of what drives you. It can also help you better understand and manage triggers and be in charge of your own emotions.

We all want to feel safe, in control and certain of ourselves and where we are headed in life. It's a natural inclination to want stability, safety and security. We need to feel comfortable in our environment and we need a sense of consistency and control. Opposite and equal to this need is the need for variety and uncertainty as well. We need to be challenged to grow, we crave excitement, surprise and adventure, change and difference. Creating that balance between the need for certainty and the need for variety can be a challenge, because if either need is not being met enough, a person will not feel satisfied. If they are too comfortable, they may end up feeling bored and not personally fulfilled. If there's too much variety, things may feel out of control and uncertain.

The more certainty we seek the more we seek to want to control everything. As a result of this behaviour, we take less risks which inhibits our chance for growth and challenge. This can lead us to feeling miserable, angry, fearful of change and lacking in self-worth. People who haven't been able to recognise that their overt need for control (or certainty), craving it like an addiction, can be destructive and counterproductive.

For example, a person who feels they don't have enough control or certainty in their lives, will seek to try and control others' and their environment to feel sustained and worthwhile. It's like they are filling up a car with petrol; the tank is themselves and the petrol for that tank is other people. They use others for their own benefit. The more they engage in this behaviour, the more it costs you to be around. By controlling their environment, by making others conform to their standards and expectations, they are in a sense temporarily 'fixing' the problem of control within themselves. It gives them a sense of importance to the degree of arrogance and is partly due to a lack of self-confidence and not fulfilling their need for certainty in a healthy, resourceful way. People who crave certainty and control at the expense of the other needs, can end up developing serious psychological disorders, one of which narcissistic behavioural tendencies stems from. The more a person craves certainty, the more fearful of change they become. The more fearful of change a person becomes, the less abundance they're likely to experience. The danger is we can stagnate if we don't keep pushing ourselves for more. The need for certainty will always be there because it occurs naturally. However, we need to be able to embrace uncertainty because the more we can handle, the more we will grow as functional human beings. It also helps boost our confidence by embracing new learnings at the same time. We become adaptable, resourceful and empowered when we aren't fearful of change and are willing to embrace the unknown with a willing spirit instead.

Take school for example. As children, when we first stepped into the school ground we were facing an uncertain environment. Just as anxious about the change were our parents/caregivers, no doubt standing beside us holding our hands in reassurance. But without embracing that uncertainty, we as children would not have been able to experience the abundance of education. Granted, at first it was scary not knowing what lay ahead, but by embracing that uncertainty, embracing the fear of the unknown, the unfamiliar became familiar.

We all need certainty in our lives but the key point is *how* we get that feeling. Do we get it by controlling others and our environment or do we get it by believing in ourselves? Ultimately the quality of life we seek will be determined by the choices we make. Do we seek to control or do we seek to embrace the unknown and expand ourselves? The more open to change we are the more growth of self we'll experience. Just like the school example, the more we embraced the uncertainty of our new educational environment, the more we grew and learned.

The more we think our environment has to change for us to feel certain the less quality of life we will have. At this point we're still looking outside ourselves to feel good. However, the more we take responsibility for our sense of certainty, the greater our feelings of self-worth and how we feel about our lives improves. It gives a person a sense of achievement, that self-determination to improve the quality of their own life if they choose to look within. Sadly, individuals who seek to change their environment and control others will never be truly happy. A way to achieve long-lasting happiness is to embrace uncertainty and not to fear the unknown anymore.

A couple of key questions to ask yourself at this stage:

1. In what ways in your own life have you been meeting this need? Has it been in a way that has enabled you to grow as a person or not?

2. What will you do to improve things?

Variety

The next human need that is a paradox of certainty, is the need for variety or adventure. Whilst we require certainty for creating healthy routines for ourselves, we also need some level of variety so we don't get bored. We are born with the desire to be challenged and learn and without embracing some level of variety, we will undoubtedly get bored. If we get bored, we start living unproductive and unfulfilling lives, leading to a sense of uneasiness. A sense of uneasiness can lead to sadness, isolation and even depression, which can make us chase quick fixes to help us feel better. These can be in the form of antidepressants or anti-anxiety pills. These quick fix measures don't sustain things, don't help create long-lasting change and are temporary only. They don't solve the problem – they mask them. Transformation, however, is not found in the bottom of a jar. It takes time, effort and commitment and is not solved simply by taking a pill.

I'm not implying that medication doesn't have a place in people's lives, that's something that only you and your doctor can decide together. What I am saying is, that using medication as a way of fixing problems is not the answer. How a person meets the need for variety, what activities they choose and what they decide to participate in says a lot about the individual.

Let's take a married couple as an example of meeting the need for variety in a healthy and mutually beneficial way or counterproductively. If things are going well in the marriage and the couple have been together for many years, creating daily routines and predictability to meet the need for certainty, how then can they meet the need for variety that doesn't damage the marriage but enhances it?

Scenario one:

A married couple has been together for years and things are going well. One of them find things are getting a little mundane, a bit too predictable and feels the need for variety, fun and excitement. The issue is they have no idea how to communicate their need effectively because they fear being rejected. The routines of ordinary life are becoming boring to them and a bit too predictable. One decides to meet this need by nit-picking constantly, leaving the other feeling drained. What started out as a small and relatively insignificant issue, has now caused unnecessary stress and has cost the quality of the relationship. One person's need for variety has just been met but at the expense of the other. Yes, it broke the status quo and changed things up a bit, but not in a positive way. The way this person's need for variety has been met has been at the cost of their partner and in the long run, could possibly damage the relationship they have with their spouse. If learned patterns of behaviour from the past are not unlearned, if the cycle of learned behaviours continues, then the quality of the marriage would be in trouble.

Scenario two:

A married couple have been together for many years and again are well and truly in routines, they know one another's habits and are very comfortable with one another. Again, the need for variety becomes important to one of them and they decide to sit down with their spouse and have a frank discussion about the issue. Because this couple are confident within themselves and are highly emotionally intelligent, having conversations around issues where they feel a need is not being met in a way they'd like is easy. The couple have created a safe place, an ability to openly communicate how they feel about things, where something may be lacking and where things are going well. The couple having discussed the issue of wanting a bit of fun and excitement in a mature, calm and mutually respectful way, make a plan to take a trip away for the weekend together and have some alone time. One of them may even decide to be spontaneous and surprise their spouse, making all the arrangements necessary so the other just needs to pack a bag and go. The point is, the need for variety in this scenario has been met in a mutually beneficial way and not in an immature, costly manner. It's more than likely that this couple will be in it together for the long haul as the space they've managed to create together is a win-win and one where open and honest discussions around their needs not being met, can be talked about without the fear of rejection.

As the above two scenarios indicate, the need for variety, for a bit of fun and excitement can be met in a functional, mutually beneficial way or in a selfish and immature way. The need for variety is important, but creating that balance, creating a safe place within a relationship where open and frank discussions can take place, is crucial for positive growth. Although extreme examples, both achieve their respective outcomes. They've met the need for variety, but only one is functional and positive.

Though it's important to understand the beauty of uncertainty, those who acknowledge it as one of their top basic human needs can take it to an extreme. They may engage in a frequent job or relationship changes for the sake of variety or take unnecessary risks to achieve the adrenaline jolt they crave. On the flip side, those who take a level-headed approach to this need, won't be afraid of taking risks and won't avoid new situations or people for the sake of comfortability. It's not being afraid of the unknown and understanding that growth exists at the edge of our comfort zone.

We all need variety, we crave adventure, fun and excitement. We need to understand that everyone's needs are different and if the need is not being met in a balanced, cohesive way it can create tension. We all have different amounts of variety we want in our lives and some people don't want a lot of uncertainty, so their need for variety is minimal. These type of people are cruising along in a middle-level role, the classic nine to five position repeating tasks over and over for years on end. These people don't want a lot of variety and are therefore perfect for the role they're in, as they are comfortable with predictability. Other people would go stir crazy in a role like that and need more variety to stay interested and stimulated. It's completely an individual choice and there's no right or wrong answer with the amount each person desires. The important thing is to recognise and understand this need and how it applies to your own life.

Ask yourself the following:

1. How much variety do I need in my life and how will I meet this need?

Significance

Another need we as human beings have is the need for significance and is probably the one need that is pivotal as an indicator of someone's level of confidence. The need for significance is met primarily through our egos, which is derived from our minds and if sought outwardly, can be tiresome and taxing on others. It is linked directly to our level of self-worth and can be met in a positive and healthy way or in an unhealthy and potentially damaging way. If the need for significance is one of your top motivators in life, a careful examination is required to see whether or not you're building a positive self-image independent of others, or whether your self-image is dependent upon what others think of you and is therefore fragile and unstable. People who have a high level of self-esteem don't need anyone else to validate them to make them feel good – it's just a bonus when they do. They don't seek out attention from others, they're not full of their own importance and are kind, humble people who seek to serve rather than be served.

People who have a low self-esteem are driven by the need for significance, as their level of self-worth hinges on what others think and say about them. As a result, that level wavers depending on what feedback they get about themselves and they crave attention. This often leads to attention-seeking behaviours such as being provocative, loud and demonstrative, being arrogant and selfish and always seeking approval from others. It's tiring to be around.

A great example of this is Donald Trump. Putting aside his political views and analysing him as a person and what motivates him, not only is he driven by money and success, but his need for significance is also a primary motivator. He seeks to dominate, to look as though he is taking the lead and has all the answers and is therefore validated as being important. He is ego-driven and proud, but he is proud at the expense of the people he is supposed to serve. You can see him literally puff up with pride when people speak publicly about him, as they stroke his ego to the extreme. He feels significant, confident and back in control, until the next time when he doesn't. If you don't believe me, watch his body language and you'll see what I'm saying is true.

People like Donald Trump who seems to have it all together, actually have low levels of self-worth. They would never admit it in a million years because their ego dictates their actions and this would be seen (by him) as being weak. The sad fact is, his confidence levels are dependent upon his 'minions' telling him what a wonderful job he is doing, what an amazing person he is and all the bells and whistles of fluffing up his ego to make him feel good. He is driven by the need to feel significant, but in an unhealthy and selfish way, that will not help build his self-esteem in a sustaining and long-lasting way. It will always waver. However, from the public's view, he *seems* to have it all. In private though, I am certain it is a very different ball game. Even then he would be keeping it hidden – even from himself.

The interesting thing is when something goes wrong, people who seek out the approval of others to meet their need, will play the victim and seek to blame others or other external factors. When something goes wrong, it is the weather's fault, it's because such and such didn't do their job properly that caused 'X' to happen and so on. Statements like this indicate a person's level of self-worth because those whose self-esteem is low, will seek to blame others for their mistakes. Even if they're partly to blame they will not take ownership, as the ego-driven individual won't allow themselves to be 'lowered' to the level of admitting to making a mistake and owning it. They see it as beneath them and people who are driven by the need for significance certainly don't make mistakes – well that's what they tell themselves anyway. It's also a sign of immaturity and an unwillingness to take responsibility for themselves and their actions.

Also on the end of low confidence levels are people who are too scared to admit they've made an error because they're fearful of letting others down. Again the opinion of others, the fear of being rejected, overrides the admission of guilt. If they're validated negatively, by being scolded or by being given a 'dressing down' for doing the wrong thing, this will undoubtedly damage the already flimsy levels of confidence and will only confirm that they're no good, useless, hopeless, etc. It upholds that belief and validates that the way they think about themselves, as poorly as they do, is warranted. To avoid that, they won't admit to doing anything wrong again, because the opinions of others in their circle of influence are so important. They'll avoid conflict at all costs, retreat into themselves and get back onto the cycle of negative self-talk again, because that person validated them and confirmed their worst fear that they're no good. When confidence levels are low, any negative feedback will be generalised and spread across other areas of life. It's taken personally.

A point I'd like to clarify with the need for validation and significance, is that the range is wide and varied and is influenced by many factors. What I mean by that is, the level of self-worth of an individual compared to another's and where that sits on the scale of measurement is not the same for every person. The behaviours a person exhibits when their confidence is low has many factors affecting it – one of which is their gender. A male whose confidence depends on the opinions and validation of others, who is ego-driven and proud, will seek out validation in a way that can be tiresome on others. He can be loud, demonstrative and overbearing, often impatient and wanting things now. He will appear to be extremely confident to those around him in his outward appearance, dominating conversations and seemingly knowing it all. It's a front. It's a mask he wears to hide his low confidence levels often being unaware even to himself that this is the cause. He *needs* the validation of others to feel significant – he craves it.

A male who has low levels of confidence does not necessarily behave outwardly the same as a female who has low levels of confidence. It is crucial to understand that males and females think and feel differently which affects how they behave. Meeting the need for validation will be different for both and will be affected and influenced by individual personality types, the way they were raised, the experiences they've encountered and if those experiences were positive or not. Gender aside for a moment, if people in general have had negative and damaging relationships with significant others, it can scar a person's confidence levels to the extreme, compelling them to seek validation in ways that they wouldn't typically do. Having said that, there are a few common indicators that remain consistent for each gender to help you understand.

Males by nature seek to be validated through their egos. Females are the opposite; they seek to have their feelings validated instead. Males like to have all the facts before them and then decide on a plan of attack to address things head-on. They'll often tell you what they *think* about a situation, rather than what they *feel* about it. Females, however, like to talk about how they feel about a situation, how it has affected them emotionally and seek comfort instead. If you asked women about a situation that has affected them so greatly, you're unlikely to get the facts about it, but rather they'll talk about how it has affected them emotionally. Understanding this primary difference for men and women is a critical aspect of effective communication and seeking to understand those differences when fulfilling the need for significance is fundamental.

For example, there is no point forcing a man to talk about how he felt about a situation, when he wants to give his opinion on the matter and tell you his thoughts instead. It's here that many women go wrong, where they miss the opportunity to validate a man's pride and confidence by not asking his opinion. What's being imposed here, is that the female driven by her desire to be compassionate, empathetic and understanding, is inadvertently forcing her needs on the male and wanting them validated. She is superimposing her expectations on him without realising it, rather than allowing him the freedom to express himself the best way he knows how. Once he has, if you want to know how he feels about a situation, ask him *after* he has given you his opinion, but respect him enough to allow him to do what he was born to do, which is to think, analyse and critique. Meeting his need for validation by meeting the needs of his ego, automatically helps build his confidence levels, whilst opening the door to honest and open communication. It builds trust.

A word of advice; don't have too many expectations around how the male in your life *should* express himself. A lot of men are not used to talking about their feelings and so it could be new territory for him. Go gently, nurturing and guiding him and validating every effort he makes however big or small they may seem. Again, baby steps and being understanding and supportive and positively reinforcing every effort, will help boost his ego and confidence as he gets used to voicing his feelings as well.

The need for significance can be met healthily through service to others, by having a giving attitude, helping others to better themselves and by having a healthy self-esteem. The higher the level of self-esteem a person has, the less they look outwardly to meet their need for significance. They're independent, strong and mature and make the best candidates for leadership, modelling excellence in all they do. People with high levels of self-confidence don't need anyone else to validate them and are comfortable taking compliments. They're independent of others and will meet this need by being proud of themselves, celebrating the success others experience and being a team-oriented person. They don't depend on others, but rather are independent of them.

The need for significance can be satisfied in a manner that contributes to your confidence levels or helps to tear them down. Being able to recognise the signs, reflect on how you interact with others and seeking to improve yourself, will ultimately contribute to the building of a positive self-esteem and higher confidence levels.

Questions to ask yourself:

1. What are some examples of meeting this need positively and healthily?

2. How are you meeting your need for significance? Are there any ways you need to improve meeting this need? If so, what will you do about it?

Connection

When a person's self-confidence and the way they view themselves are at their best, a person is ready for loving another human being selflessly. The need for connection – for love, is a natural trait we've all been gifted with. Unfortunately, not a lot of people are driven by the purity of it and don't see it as a primary motivator. Every human being on the planet needs love. This need for connection can also be met healthily and happily or the complete opposite is true. We can meet this need in various ways that can either add value to ours and others lives or the complete opposite is true. Another important aspect when talking about love is the intention behind this driver.

We can meet the need for love and connection by being in a loving relationship, by praying, talking, exercising, writing and so on. Whatever the heart desires, whatever a person's primary motivators and interests are, those will propel them forward to meet this need in that way. That's not to say that someone who loves to pray will only pray or someone who loves to write will only write. It isn't at the exclusion of everything else – it's not an all or nothing type concept. It's a giving, selfless act, one that will satisfy a person's need for love in unimaginable ways. When a person is driven by love in all that they do, then the actions they take will enhance their own and others' lives who are around them.

A person who knows themselves well – knows their strengths and knows what areas they need to improve will be proactive by nature. People like this are driven by an internal standard and a level of confidence that allows them to not be affected by what others' opinions of them are. Their ability to accept themselves (faults and all), to forgive self and others and ultimately love themselves to the best of their ability, will then be reflected outwardly in their behaviours and interactions with others.

People like this constantly smile, they always look for the good in any situation and are not bound by others' expectations. These people are the ones who are ready to be in a long-term committed loving relationship, as they don't *need* the validation of others to make them feel good – they already do. They've done the hard yards, they have examined events from the past, they've reached that stage where nothing holds them back and they've managed to break the ball and chain of pain and heartache that once held them captive. They're givers and not takers. Their ability to love and to love selflessly is what we all strive to be like and loving yourself is the most important step to take in achieving internal satisfaction and happiness. Learning to love and accept yourself completely means your focus isn't on needing someone else to complete you, but rather wanting someone else to compliment you.

Confidence levels have a direct link to a person's ability to love and to love in the best intended way – selflessly. Sadly, for some, when a woman who appears to be confident by wearing the latest fashion, loads of makeup and the high heels to match, she may just be projecting an image of confidence. In actuality, what she may be doing is hiding away what's really going on inside. The outward projection of being presented the best she can, seeking the validation of others that she looks good, may not be a true reflection of what is going on internally. In a lot of cases women who are hell-bent on projecting an image of so-called perfection, have actually got low levels of self-worth.

In such cases the version of themselves that they are presenting to the world may be very different from that of their core selves. The issue with the makeup and fashion obsession is that if it's being used to mask what's going on underneath the surface, then there's a problem that needs dealing with. If the makeup is being used to mask pain and heartache of previous years of being rejected and hurt, it's an indication of an unwillingness to be vulnerable or 'exposed' again. Needing makeup as a crutch to make ourselves feel good is not in line with being centred and whole as a person. There's an underlying issue with confidence levels that have undoubtedly been the result of negative interactions with significant others, that have had a lasting impact personally.

To illustrate my point, I used to use makeup as a way of making myself feel good because people always told me how pale and sick I looked. I was also told I looked prettier with loads of makeup on, so it was a natural thought for me to think that I needed it to feel important enough to warrant attention from others. Eventually I worked out that I had been relying on the validation of others to feel good about myself. My confidence levels were so low, I needed to heal from those years of being told I wasn't attractive and was sickly looking and find that part of myself where I was truly comfortable with who I was.

I'm certainly not indicating that using makeup is wrong in any way – not at all. A little makeup can enhance a woman's natural features giving her a sense of pride and reinforces her belief about herself that she doesn't need copious amounts to feel good. However, I believe that if it's being used as a way of projecting an air of confidence that isn't a direct reflection of her core self and *needs* the praises of others to boost her confidence levels, then she is suffocating her core and not allowing that part of her to be exposed. It is a problem. She is relying on others to validate her and to feel significant as she hasn't yet learned how to love and accept herself. Healing that inner part only comes when we allow that part of ourselves to once again be exposed, but under very different circumstances than previously.

My point is, if the version we as women present to the world is very different to the version of ourselves that is not in the public eye and we need external measures such as makeup or fashion accessories to make us feel good, then that's a major issue. Having two versions becomes tiresome and draining and in reality, who wants a life where we've got to constantly remember what version we need to present and in what context? Deep down this desire for acceptance is a result of a fear of being rejected again, which stems from past experiences of not being loved when we were vulnerable and exposed. We weren't loved unconditionally. Is it any wonder some of us have felt the need to cover and protect ourselves!

Again, the feedback she gets and when she gets it will reinforce her own set of beliefs about herself. The connection and love she craves eludes her until such a point of self-acceptance. What she doesn't realise, are those times when the positive reinforcement she got that were linked to the fake eyelashes, the short dress and so on, only goes to confirm that she needs to look a certain way to be loved and accepted. She seeks to be desired, but is being desired in the wrong way. It may sound harsh, but women who seek such attention tend to say they want to be respected for their brains and not their bodies, yet the image they project is quite the opposite. Men naturally are attracted to the naked skin and the shapely bodies they see, so it's a little hard for them to not look upon a woman in a lustful, sensual way. Yes, we all want to be desired, but we don't want to be desired by the masses – just that special someone in our life.

On the other side of the coin when she's going about her daily routines and tending to the family's needs, she won't necessarily be dressed to the 'nines'. More than likely, she'd be wearing (for example), jeans and a t-shirt and little to no makeup. If she is not getting any positive reinforcement for the way she looks now that is genuine, it goes to confirm that in her natural state she isn't worthy of the kind of love that accepts her naturally. Her ability to accept herself is based almost entirely on the opinion of others. That's what validates her – good or bad and seeking this externally doesn't build confidence. It cripples it. The love and connection she desires escapes her clutches and so she feels she needs to 'dress to impress' to be validated and build her confidence back up again.

It's in these moments in her natural state, that the ultimate validation of being complimented makes the most impact and can help improve how she feels about herself. If she doesn't seek approval nor relies on others to validate her, then it's at this stage in her life that she is ready for love. When her complete acceptance of herself is at its peak, her ability to love others without any ulterior motive than to simply love without condition is at its best. She will not have the ability to commit to the relationship with passion, honesty and most importantly in a giving and selfless way, until she can love and accept herself first.

Let's look at 'Married at First Sight' – the Channel Nine series about couples who meet for the first time at the alter and are married within a few minutes. The whole idea of the show is for couples to fall in love and live happily ever after guided by experts and life coaches. What we see happen in reality and why many of the couples have issues in their marriage, is in part due to the individuals involved not knowing and loving themselves enough first, to know what it is they truly desire. Are the qualities they seek in a partner superficial? Are the qualities they seek in the other the core set of values, principles and beliefs similar to their own?

If the latter is true and the partner they get matched with has similar beliefs and expectations, then the marriage is off to a good start. If, however, it is based on what a person looks like, what job they do and how much they earn, then it's likely that there'll be a mismatch in values. It's unlikely two people would be driven primarily by money and success at the expense of love (in a social experiment such as this). Again, the whole idea is to fall in love and fall in love with an open heart and the right intentions and many of the 2020 couples fell short. Many couples were married off with a mismatch of intentions and driving forces, causing unnecessary arguments and ultimately separation occurred.

The show is a great learning tool for how *not* to behave in a relationship. Most of the 2020 participants came into the experiment with either relationship baggage, issues with confidence or the wrong motives altogether. It's interesting to watch the dynamics involved and almost every couple has had major communication issues. One of the participants, Connie, wanted a husband because she didn't want to be lonely anymore. She stated on many occasions that she lacked confidence and wanted to be with someone out of fear of being alone. Connie was looking at things from a fear-based perspective.

As the weeks unfolded, Connie had been eager to please, had lost herself in the process and stated on a number of occasions, 'I just want to be loved.' The issue for her partner Jonnie, was that he could see that she *needed* him to feel good about herself. She desperately sought to feel confident within herself and was far from being ready for a loving, committed relationship. Week by week she slowly began building her confidence, but the building shouldn't happen within the marriage – that work needs to be done beforehand. Yes, within the marriage one's confidence grows absolutely, but to come into a marriage with little to no confidence is not the way to begin a lifelong union. The need for connection and love is natural, but to take it to the level of committing oneself to another person for the rest of your life in a healthy and sustaining way, you need to know and love yourself completely first to give your best in the relationship. Otherwise, you're doing a disservice to yourself and your partner.

The wonderful thing out of all of these realisations Connie had, was that she needed to grow as a person. The Connie that began the experiment to the Connie that finished it was completely different. She had remarked at the amount of confidence she now had, how she found strength and freedom to be herself and not shy away from interacting with others. By the end of the show a confident, strong, beautiful and unique individual stood before him and she left feeling empowered. Even though they didn't end up being married, the journey of self-discovery for Connie over the eight or nine weeks, gave her a new sense of identity and purpose and the confidence to know what she wanted in life. She was a new person.

The need to be connected to something or someone can be done well or in a completely self-destructive way. It's an individual choice how we meet the need for love and connection, but it's a need we all have. Recognising what is healthy, recognising whether you're loving the wrong things, takes self-reflection and trusting your instincts as well. Quite often when we do something that doesn't feel right, we get a sense of uneasiness in the pit of our stomach. This is nature's way of telling us to stop doing what we're doing. It's an inbuilt mechanism to help us recognise what is good for us and what isn't. Great examples of these are alcohol abuse, drug-taking and anti-social behaviours.

Love and connection stem from this instinct and being self-aware, recognising your strengths and areas for growth, are critical for long term happiness. Your need for love starts with you and being able to look yourself in the mirror and say positive things about yourself. It's a great indication of your confidence levels too. It's being self-aware enough to not be arrogant, selfish or greedy, but to be humble, kind and selfless. When you know yourself well and can accept and love all the unique talents and abilities you have, you won't accept or take on the criticism of others. You'll have the ability to recognise that the poison they sprout forth is a reflection of what's going on inside *them* and not you. You'll stand your ground and be able to speak up and not allow their poison to affect how you feel about yourself.

Ask yourself the following questions. Write down your thoughts and be honest with yourself.

1. Have I been hiding my true self away through fear of being rejected? If so, how can I change this?

2. How have the choices I've made lately affected my relationships?

3. How can I meet my need for love and connection healthily?

Growth

The fifth need is growth. Growth is optional and is an individual's decision whether or not they embrace this need or not, but it's a large factor in determining the level of happiness a person feels. You don't have to grow, it's entirely up to you, but it will ultimately affect the level of happiness and sense of satisfaction you feel in the long run.

If we grow, we feel good about ourselves, our self-worth goes up and our confidence builds. It's like when you first learn how to operate a manual car and you practice and practice until it becomes automatic. Your ability to learn and stick at it until you grasp exactly how to change the gears, gives you a sense of achievement and accomplishment. This is growth. It's the ability to embrace something new, to learn new and better ways of doing things, which will contribute to your well-being.

Growth is larger than learning how to change the gears in a manual car. It's evolving, learning and growing that helps not only you to improve, but it will then have a flow-on effect and help others too. It's a natural part of being human to want to pass on knowledge that helps others. Without growth being part of our everyday lives this simply won't happen.

If we aren't growing we become stagnant, stuck in a rut and going through the motions of life. This level of satisfaction is shallow – it isn't sustaining and is not satisfying. People who are in this situation waste their time doing mundane things like watching a lot of television, do not use their spare time well and won't have a high self-esteem. They waste time participating in activities that don't give them any real sense of satisfaction or pride and are in denial about their true purpose in life.

Perhaps they haven't discovered that yet, perhaps they haven't taken the time to uncover it, but without starting to embrace their gifts and recognise their talents, their personal growth and development will remain stagnant. It simply won't happen. People like this will continue to go through the motions without knowing who they are as a person and without any real sense of identity.

The idea behind growth is to expand our core selves. It's like when we went to school as children. At first, the idea of school was pretty overwhelming, scary and exciting at the same time, but the amount of growth we experienced was astronomical. If someone told you from the age of five to the age of seventeen that you would know the amount of knowledge you know now back then, you'd never have believed it. It probably would have frightened you too. However, that's the beauty of growth; it's learning new things to improve ourselves and as a natural by-product, will help improve the lives of others as well.

The idea behind growth is to keep expanding our core knowledge because without growth we can shrink our core. It's like not exercising. If we are not using our minds and we aren't challenging it, rehearsing things and learning new skills, then our brain begins to contract with the amount of knowledge it has. The application of that knowledge gets forgotten, so growth is a huge need in all of us. We all need to exercise our brain as much as our body if it's to stay in its optimal shape. This is growth at its best.

Something for you to consider:

1. In what area/s of your life do you need to grow?

2. What steps can you implement to make growth in those areas a reality?

Contribution

The sixth and final need is contribution. I'm going to go out on a limb to say there's a seventh need but more on that later. Contribution, like growth is optional; you don't have to contribute to the growth and development of others – it's entirely your own decision to make. But contributing to other people's lives in a meaningful and positive way, funnily enough, meets some of your own needs as well. Your own need for significance, validation and connection are met and contributing to others' lives gives you a great deal of satisfaction.

Contribution helps the person who gives it to grow and to feel certainty as well. The recipient feels validated and their need for growth is being met in a meaningful and positive way. Contribution combined with growing personally and professionally, is the best way to feel great about yourself.

Here's where it gets really interesting. If any behaviour you are currently doing meets three out of the six core needs, you become addicted to that behaviour. Whether it is good for you or not, you'll continue to repeat the same patterns even if it is harmful. We see this type of thing happen when people partake in anti-social behaviour and surround themselves with like-minded people. If the group continue to do the actions they do and are validated by others in the group, then it will continue. Even if the validation is negative by normal standards, such as egging one another on to graffiti a wall, the need is being met. The need of feeling certain by controlling others' actions, the need for variety by 'playing up' and the need for connection by being in the group are all being met. As mentioned, if at least three of those needs are met, then this cycle of anti-social behaviour will undoubtedly continue. The needs for certainty, variety, connection and significance are all being met – four out of the six core needs. It's when individuals recognise that their need for growth and contribution (the two needs that *aren't* being met) become a priority, that things will begin to change.

The best way to correct this negative pattern is to become aware of how it is affecting you personally and how it's meeting your needs. Once you become aware that the way you've been meeting your needs hasn't been serving you positively and productively, you can then begin the process of replacing those behaviours with alternate ones that do serve you. Realising that things have to change, that life isn't turning out to be all that you'd hoped for, the process of taking on new learnings and new understandings can now begin.

When we embrace change, embrace these new learnings, our other needs start getting met at the same time – but in a healthy and positive way. The only way we can meet the need for contribution is to meet our other needs first. To find new learnings, new understandings in how we can be more productive and contributing members of society, is where we aim to be.

To break old thinking patterns and their respective behaviours takes awareness of self. Human beings have inbuilt mechanisms that make them seek out the feelings of being validated and important. We all want to feel loved and to feel connected and we need a sense of certainty and variety as well. As a result of this, we feel the need to expand, to grow and to learn. But if these needs are being met negatively, it goes against the very core of who we are. That's why people who display behaviours that are socially unacceptable are really crying out for help. They have not yet learned acceptable and productive ways of getting help, because if they knew how to, they'd already be doing it. Their anti-social antics are their way of getting attention, a way of being connected to others, but if they don't reach a stage where they honour their core values and seek out happiness, the result will ultimately be a life that is less than satisfying and feelings of worthlessness and sadness will follow.

We get addicted to behaving in a certain way because it meets our needs whether healthily or in an unfulfilling way. If a person loves to gossip they'll continue gossiping – if it meets three of their needs (variety in what they say, connection with others and feeling significant by spreading the gossip). However, if that person who loves to gossip isn't surrounded by the same type of people and does not get the validation they seek, then the pattern of behaviour will cease. Their needs are not being met, so they'll either seek out others who are like-minded to continue that pattern of behaviour or eventually realise that their gossiping ways aren't serving them. If a person does not get the validation they seek with discouraging responses, it may just be the spark that lights the flame of self-belief and stops that behaviour from continuing.

The idea is that people need to surround themselves with a better quality of friendships. Once the spark has been lit and the light of realisation has been turned on, a person needs to honour their self-worth and continue down the road of self-improvement. It's recognising you are worth it and deserve a better quality of life, that these types of conversations have done absolutely nothing to serve or help you (or anyone else for that matter). The point comes when you need to ask yourself, what's the point in them anyway? How are the conversations I'm having helping me live a rewarding and happy life? They aren't.

The choice is yours and yours alone and that's the key point; it's a choice of how you decide to live. Some people fall into the trap of having the victim mentality of constantly reminding others just how tough they have it, that the choice in the matter was taken away from them and that the decision on how they are choosing to live has already been made. I understand that financial resources can be an inhibiting factor in propelling a person forward to attaining their ultimate dream, but that shouldn't be the determining factor that holds a person back. It has to start somewhere. It's a step at a time and not a giant leap. The goal of attainment may seem like a pipe dream away, but is a step by step process. As the saying goes, 'Rome wasn't built in a day'. It takes planning, preparation and decisive action to change our lives for the better and it all starts with the choices you make and whether you want a better life for yourself or not. It's up to you. It's that simple.

The God Factor – the seventh need

As I mentioned earlier, I believe we have a seventh human need that is instinctively within us all. I like to call it the God factor. Some people might term it as spirituality, which I don't have an issue with, but I do believe it is worthy of being included as a basic human need. We all have a part of our brain that scientists have discovered that is simply for worship and the only way the blood supply reaches the area at the front of the brain is when we bow our heads in a downward fashion. For some people, this may seem a little controversial (which I never shy away from), but I wouldn't include it if it wasn't a scientific fact.

We all have a desire to find higher meaning in life, that purpose as mentioned, but it goes further than that. Every person is born with a living soul, that part of us that isn't clothed with skin and bone, but the very essence of who we are. It has its own need to be fulfilled and sustained and is a huge factor in determining the level of happiness a person feels in life.

All of us at one stage or another have asked ourselves the universal questions, why am I here? What's the purpose of life? What's the purpose of creation? In some way shape or form, questions such as these have haunted people since the dawn of time until they found the answers they sought for themselves. This need can be fulfilled in a meaningful and purposeful way or a self-destructive, unfulfilling and miserable way. Honouring what's innate, honouring your natural-born instinct to find deeper meaning, to find that higher purpose, drives every living soul whether we are aware of it or not. Being aware of it, allows a person to fulfil the desires and needs of the soul that ultimately leads to true happiness and a sense of peace.

I liken it to an upside-down triangle with the soul being the tip of the triangle that is firmly planted in the ground. It's the tip that carries all the other needs and without that central force, that stabilised grounded point, a human being wanders around aimlessly through life and the rest of the needs become meaningless and unsustaining. Without that central force (a living soul within us), life would be completely meaningless and is therefore, the most crucial need of all to fulfil.

The soul is connected to our brains, our heartfelt desires and the feelings of uneasiness we get when we do something wrong is going against the soul. The saying, 'do what your heart and soul desires' is applicable here too, because if we don't honour that, we get these feelings like something's off and a sense that we are wasting time in meaningless activities.

So the purpose of having a soul is to guide us in our everyday lives. Again, envisage an upside-down triangle with it holding all the other needs up; without listening to it, life becomes meaningless, empty and shallow. It leads to boredom and participating in activities that don't bring us joy, contentment and a sense of pride. It leads us down the path of feeling bad about ourselves and contributes to having low self-esteem and confidence levels.

It begs the question therefore, who placed a soul within us and why did they care so much about us to give us that internal compass? If we were created to live life to the fullest and to reach our highest potential, it warrants mentioning at least who created us and why.

Human experience and simple logic tell us that something that has a beginning, does not simply come from nothing nor can something create itself. Therefore, the most rational explanation is that there must be a creator that initiated everything and not just us, but also the universe as we know it. People have different views on this subject and that's fine – each to his own. However, since I have taken the path of wanting to know the truth and answer those all-important universal questions, I found the answer in Islam.

Without going into too much detail, I must admit I had to put aside my preconceived notions and ideas I had about Islam, formed largely as a result of what the media had portrayed. I had quite a harsh judgement about what I thought Islam was about without really knowing the facts. It was all assumptions and conjecture that had formed my stance and view on the religion. However, once I put aside those misconceptions, what I discovered was the complete opposite. Islam is nothing like what I had once believed. It is a beautiful, peaceful way of life that teaches all the fundamentals of life that were important to me. It was a journey that began a few years ago and continues until this day, but one that has proven to be the best decision of my life. My desire to find God, The Creator, The Universal One, whatever you decide to call Him, was what fuelled my desire to keep going until I found the truth.

This 'being' must be powerful and intelligent enough that they're capable of bringing the whole universe into existence and create the laws of science which govern it as well. Because the Creator creates beings, we can conclude that this higher power is timeless and is not bound by time, space or having a beginning or an end – they've always been. Being human, it is sometimes difficult to grasp the concept of a being not having a start or an end, but the signs of creation are all around us and can only be explained this way.

Imagine walking in a desert and finding a watch. We know a watch consists of glass, plastic and metal. Glass comes from sand, plastic from oil and metal extracted from the ground. All these components are found in the desert. Would you believe that the watch formed itself? That the sun shone, the wind blew, lightning struck, the oil bubbled to the surface and mixed with the sand and metal and over millions of years? That the watch then came together by random or natural coincidences? Of course not. It had to be created.

Naturally, some will retort by asking, well who created God? The very question itself defies logic, because if the Creator creates something, He cannot be created. God is eternal, has always existed and has no beginning or end. That's just the way it is.

Therefore, God who created us all so uniquely and with an individual personality, size, shape, colour and of course a soul, needs at the very minimum acknowledgement. He gave us a soul as a guide for life to help us live the happiest, most loving and self-sustaining lives possible. Without honouring our souls' needs without 'tuning into it', the rest become meaningless. It's our internal compass, our guide in life and we need to learn better and more sustainable ways to live life purposefully, if we want to create a life of our choosing that is meaningful.

Tool 8

Sacrifice vs Selfishness

"Putting yourself first doesn't mean you don't care about others. It means you're smart enough to know you can't help others if you don't help yourself first."

Simple Reminders

When we talk about putting ourselves first, quite often the wrong thoughts come to mind. In Western society in particular, putting yourself first is viewed as being selfish and perhaps even arrogant as well. This is understandable of course, because a lot of the rich and powerful have attained the positions they have, because they've done so at the expense of others and without a second thought of who they've had to step on in the process. They have put themselves first, but in the wrong way. It may seem like they have it all, but when it's all said and done – they don't. They've paid a personal cost for their fame and fortune.

Many of these people in their personal lives feel miserable and lonely. Chasing accolades, fame and glory it all comes at the expense of internal security and peace of mind. It's sad but true, that many in these positions who have put their own needs before others, at the expense of others, don't feel a sense of certainty within. There's an inner turmoil they often cannot explain and it is in part due to being selfish. They feel a sense of uneasiness, that at any given moment their wealth and fortune could be taken away and always seem to be on guard. The problem is they're doing exactly that; guarding and not opening themselves up for love, genuine peace and security and their levels of self-worth and confidence levels suffer as a result.

It may seem like they're confident, it may seem like they have it all, but in reality all they have is stuff. Collections of material wealth that does nothing to help them feel truly sustained or at peace with themselves and having climbed the ladder of success the way they have, it creates a sense of uneasiness within. Celebrities spend years and likewise dollars, to find out what is missing from their lives, not understanding it is their own choices that have cost them. Not that they would publicly admit to feeling this way, but it is true. Success attained at the expense of others is the very definition of selfishness.

The difficulty is that these are usually the types of role models that are thrust into the limelight, strewn across social media, television screens and so on. The glitz and glamour of the screen, the public facade is simply a smokescreen to cover what's going on behind closed doors. Behind closed doors, many celebrities are in a world of pain, too scared or too arrogant to admit that there's a problem, because the public face becomes what's most important. They're afraid of letting others down or afraid of losing their success and look at life through the lens of fear. Sacrificing their internal happiness and sense of peace becomes the norm and thus the cycle of negativity and feeling miserable continues in order to please the masses.

The other issue is they haven't grown up. They haven't learned what true responsibility means and continue to rely on others to run their lives for them. It's comfortable, it's easy and, therefore, doesn't require much maturity in the lives they lead.

Many high rollers work so hard that they end up burning themselves out and their family life is almost non-existent. Their focus is money and power and it is this that drives them. It also costs them. The hidden costs don't have a monetary value and yet it happens to be the costliest thing of all – their relationships with significant others and with themselves suffer the most. The high incidents of heart attacks, disease and early deaths due to overworking and stress that's been left unmanaged are shockingly high. The balance in their lives, the so-called work/life balance almost doesn't exist. Most of their time is spent at work and if not physically present at the company, are on the phone or sending late-night emails. Time that could have been spent exercising, reading or with family members has eluded them.

I'd like to share an excerpt from a book I highly recommend reading titled, *High Performance Habits* (p91 by Brendon Burchard). The following illustrates my point very well and is a great example of what *not* to do:

"If I keep up this pace, I'll eventually burn out, or probably just die."

Arjun laughs and shifts uncomfortably in his chair. "Then all this was for nothing."

He looks as though he's barely slept in months. His face sags. His eyes are red, the sparkle inside gone. He doesn't have the vibrant charge like he did on the cover of that business magazine last year.

I feign a look of surprise. "Die, huh. When do you think 'eventually' might happen? Are we talking next week? This year? Next year?"

"I'm not sure. But don't tell anyone."

It's brave of him to be telling me this. No one likes to admit they've been working themselves into the ground. Especially here in Silicon Valley, it's a badge of honour to work nonstop. There are a lot of young, smart workaholics here on this peninsula, pumped up on excessive caffeine and become-a-billionaire-in-a-few-years dreams."

The story goes onto talk about the executive and the cost of his decisions to himself and also to his wife and family. What Arjun didn't want to admit, was that it was his own choices that were the cause and not the environment he was in. The environment of success at all costs, the mindset of win-lose and not win-win and the personal cost to his health, was already telling on his face. All the accolades in the world couldn't help take away the fact that his lifestyle choices and his work ethic were costing him more than he had anticipated.

What's interesting to note, is that even when the obvious is pointed out to him by life coach Brendon Burchard, that he is tired, that he is working at an insane pace, that the tell-tale signs of utter tragedy are just around the corner, he still looked for the quick fixes. When executives like Arjun work on schedules that are high-paced and high pressure, it has to cost something. In this case, Arjun's health was beginning to suffer and his choices were affecting other aspects of his life as well. When people want success at all costs, they do pay a price for wanting it all. They create this mindset that everything must happen now and haven't developed the ability to delay gratification, seeking instead the easy quick-fire solutions. They want instant results and instant solutions to problems and are impatient by nature. That there is the issue.

Arjun was pumping himself with injections of B vitamins, was not getting enough sleep, burning the candle at both ends and was not exercising. Sheer rest of mind and body were completely out of the equation and the signs of an early heart attack were already there. Arjun's lifestyle choices serve as a great example of what can happen if we allow circumstances to dictate our actions. If we are not mature and wise enough to recognise we require change, then an early death sentence is the likely outcome. Quick fixes just don't work. The longing for sustainability that's healthy and productive, that nurtures the cries of the heart and soul are the keys to success. Everything else is simply a bonus.

These lifestyle choices also have a ripple effect within the work environment as well. When the boss is showing signs of lethargy is quick-tempered and demanding, it creates a sense of uneasiness in the workplace. Team spirit is down, effective communication becomes non-existent and a general sense of negativity and lack of productivity are the result. People don't work well in an environment that is not conducive to their talents, that doesn't embrace their differences and has placed a halt on professional development. Because our lifestyle choices go further than impacting us personally, it becomes an even greater priority for those in leadership positions to be demonstrating the right type of choices and modelling excellence in all they do. After all, every decision we make and every action we take is a choice and with those choices comes much responsibility.

It's difficult to have genuine respect for individuals who have inherited their wealth or attained their position in business using unscrupulous methods. Western society has the mentality that unless you've worked hard for your money to have what you have you don't deserve it. It places a great deal of value on the effort people put in to attain their positions and not on the title itself. You might be the President or Manager of a corporation because you inherited it, but so what. Respect is earned and not just expected in this instance. Some might even say it is the very definition of selfishness.

I have seen several interviews of famous people who've been in Hollywood, who've crashed and burned and spoken publicly about how miserable they felt. They spoke about how Hollywood chewed them up and spat them out and all their hopes and dreams came crashing down around them. What they longed for, what they were searching for, was not the neon lights of Vegas, but what was hidden deep within them. Sadly, they just didn't know how to tap into that and then spent the next umpteen years undoing the damage that fame and fortune cost them. Not the ideal role models of making a difference and making their fortune the right way. The price it cost them was far too high.

So who are the type of people we should aspire to be like? Who models excellence and creativity and makes a difference in the lives of others? Who attains their respective positions by putting themselves first the right way and are role models for life? Who then, do we look to?

People like teachers, doctors, nurses, veterinarians, firefighters, plumbers, entrepreneurs, small business owners and so on. People that are in their chosen field because they had a desire to help others and honour their own calling in life. These type of people have worked hard, spent years getting the right qualifications for their respective careers and have planned and prepared for their future selves.

They have chased their dreams – have sacrificed the parties, the expensive dinners and dream holidays because their eyes were fixed firmly on the prize. They knew the road to achieving success was long and at times arduous, which came at the expense of distractions and not at the expense of themselves or others. The things they may have sacrificed to get where they are replaceable. They are material or superficial and don't cost them personal happiness or fulfilment. Personal happiness and fulfilment is irreplaceable and is therefore of greater value and cannot be sacrificed.

Those who've achieved this type of success have gone without luxury items, have not entertained selfish desires or given into tempting distractions, but have put their needs of accomplishment and achievement first in order to be successful. Without putting themselves first in this instance, they wouldn't be in the position to help others or make a positive impact either. It's a healthy selfishness. Without these types of positive role models, we wouldn't have the society we do today. It's these everyday people who are making a difference in the lives of others we should want to be like. They've earned our respect and not simply demanded it.

I know my greatest role model was my mother. She was an excellent primary school teacher, who oozed excellence and professionalism and who knew the meaning of the word sacrifice. I remember her telling me stories of how with very little money to go to college, she would ride her moped in the freezing cold wintery snow to get her education. Separated from her own family and having to board at a very young age, she put aside all her desires and her wants in life because she knew she needed the education to become the teacher she was. It was her example, her excellence and her willingness to sacrifice all else to better herself, that inspired me to become a teacher as well. We both had a passion for education, a passion for personal growth and development and a passion to mould and change the lives of countless individuals. It's here in the educational setting, my passion to help people create better lives for themselves first began.

Having said all that, it runs so much deeper and understanding when to sacrifice and when to put ourselves first is crucial. We cannot afford to sacrifice ourselves in order to please other people, as this doesn't lead to happiness, but a life of regret and even feelings of guilt. It can also lead a person to have a grudge against the people they have sacrificed for, if they don't learn to take care of themselves first. People can be left feeling like they've missed out on things because they've continuously sacrificed for others leaving them feeling unfulfilled and even resentful.

As a personal coach and mentor, I have seen this type of thing many times. As women, we have been socially trained to believe that when we put our wants and needs first we are being selfish. We are taught that our worth is based on our ability and willingness to consistently put others' needs before our own. We have been led to believe that when we choose to honour our inner desires it is selfish behaviour. These beliefs have caused so many of us to feel guilty, to question ourselves, to deny our own happiness and set up relationships as one-way streets, leaving us feeling empty and devoid of true happiness. These beliefs have not served us well.

A great example of sacrificing self to please someone else was Michelle from the Channel Nine television series, 'Married at First Sight' 2020. Michelle married a guy named Steve, who told her during the experiment that he was not attracted to her in an intimate sense, but that he loved her. They had formed what seemed a very strong bond, but that's as far as it went. Michelle found herself confused and had lost her sense of self to please Steve. He would tell her how much he cared for her, how he couldn't imagine his life without her, yet his actions said the opposite. She was left feeling bewildered and lacking in confidence. She had sacrificed her desire for a loving and intimate husband to please him. These mixed signals he constantly gave her, had her questioning herself and whether or not she was an attractive and worthwhile person and she was in desperate need of independent help.

When the couple parted ways before the final commitment ceremony, they had a week to think about whether or not to continue as husband and wife outside the show. For Michelle, this time was critical. She needed the help of her family and close friends to give her advice about whether to continue or not. She had lost herself so much that she almost needed to be told what to do.

There was a moment when she was speaking with her daughter and sister around the kitchen table and after discussing the main aspects of her and Steve's relationship, Michelle had a light bulb moment. She said something to the effect that she felt as if electromagnetic thoughts were popping up left, right and centre and a moment of clarity resulted. She suddenly realised that she had forgotten her own needs and they had taken a back seat to the needs of Steve. She realised that she had not remained true to herself and had placed his needs, sacrificially before her own.

That moment helped Michelle make her final decision on whether to stay in the marriage or to go. This scene was followed by Michelle sitting in a rainforest to give her the clarity she needed to write her final vows. It was here she was able to honour her own needs and find her voice again. Her confidence and self-esteem levels were in tatters and it was by removing herself from the busyness of the show, that she was able to draw the strength to remind herself that she was worthy of so much more, than what she had settled for.

At the final commitment ceremony, an unaware and quite frankly clueless Steve, expected that Michelle would write stay and that he would continue the relationship outside the experiment. Throughout the entire series, we had seen a self-absorbed Steve project one thing and his actions said another. He was trying to convince everyone that his feelings for Michelle (which I believe were genuine in the sense of a deep friendship), could develop into more. Contrary to this, was his statement to Michelle earlier in the series, that he was 'not attracted to her physically' which left Michelle feeling heartbroken.

I believe he was trying to convince himself that he could love her more than just a friend, to save face publicly and not look ridiculous sprouting forth puff and wind affirmations. His juvenile ways, his immature emotional and mental capacities, continued throughout the entire experiment. He was dominating in conversations and was not attuned to listening with empathy or accustomed to wanting to understand others' points of view. When Michelle did get the courage up to talk about how she was feeling with him, she was met with defensive and self-justifying answers, that left her feeling not validated and not heard. She had to take a stand and put herself first. She had to remember that it was okay to put her own needs first before his, that it was okay to be selfish. A healthy, much needed selfish.

Michelle wrote leave at the final ceremony and told him exactly what she wanted. She finally gave her feelings and emotions a voice and by doing so, she had regained her strength. Michelle walked away from the ceremony empowered and strong, standing tall and confident and her dignity and self-worth intact. She had handled the situation with class and style and had finally put herself first. Michelle quickly learned to stop the old habits of sacrificing her own happiness in order to please others and now understood the meaning behind putting herself first. She had stopped the cycle of needless sacrifice once and for all.

Learning to put yourself first – developing healthy selfishness, is the key to achieving what you want in your life. If you're ruled and governed by others and what they need and want, it will be one of the barriers that prevents you from achieving what you set your sights on. If you don't focus on what you want because you're so busy doing things for others, thinking and worrying about what others think of you – then you need to get more selfish. You're not going to let anyone down. You're not being mean or cruel. You have a right to be happy like everyone else and frankly, it isn't your job to make them happy either. That's their job!

People often get concerned about what others will think of them if they suddenly stop running around after them and getting involved in other people's business. They don't focus on what they want because they don't have the time left to dedicate a portion for themselves. They're so used to being involved with stuff that isn't that important, that it's become habitual. If it's a habit then that's an issue, as it takes a consistent, committed effort to implement a new habit to replace an old one. Formed patterns of behaviour are very hard to break, but it can happen if you're willing to acknowledge that your needs, your hopes and your dreams, don't deserve to be put aside for the sake of others and that you deserve to prioritise them. They need to become your new focus.

Secondly, sometimes we fear the judgement of others, particularly when it comes to a possible career change. I know for some of my clients who are wives and mothers this is particularly prevalent and applicable to them. For many of us who are in the age group of forty to fifty-five years, a career change and a complete shift of focus can happen during this time. When children are either young independent adults or living out of the home entirely and we're suddenly left with an empty nest, it can be a distressing time. This new-found lifestyle where all the years of devoting ourselves to our families and putting their needs first, has created a gap in routine and time on our hands. How we deal with this new found freedom will determine the quality of life we will then experience.

It's when this realisation happens that the role of being a mother isn't what it was before, that we can find ourselves wondering what to do. We had sacrificed for many years, putting the needs of others first (and rightly so when it comes to raising a family), but now the balance has shifted and a re-examination and adjustment is in order, if internal peace and security are to return. It's time to get selfish. It's time to get excited and open doors to possibilities and find new dreams. The time for sacrificing ourselves is over.

Learning to say yes to the things that matter to you will build your self-confidence. It's a time to get creative, to explore new options and above all, keep a positive mindset when tackling anything new. How you view these new opportunities and free time is critical, as the complete opposite can occur with some feeling lost, confused, isolated and even depressed. This can end up affecting the very core of ourselves and our identity can take a battering. Being aware of the trap of negativity, being aware of these cues that can either take a positive road or a negative one, the hope is you'll be tooled up ready to tackle the next phase of your life – your own needs.

Constantly putting off your decisions because of old patterns of wanting to keep the peace will erode your self-confidence. It can even fester internally and create a sense of begrudgement and self-pity. This can lead to some women seeking attention to validate themselves in an attempt to build their self-confidence, but building confidence based on the opinions of others is flimsy at best. As people come and go, so does their opinion of you, which in turn, harms your self-worth because it creates instability and even an identity crisis.

When you communicate who you are and what you want, people around you relax because they know what you stand for. People are drawn to others who are self-assured and find it attractive as well. For single women this is a major attraction for men. Men love a self-assured woman who knows herself and knows what she wants in life and sets out to achieve it. They love it because they realise you won't rely solely on them for validation to keep your self-worth intact. Men don't like needy women. Men love to be wanted – not needed. Being self-assured and knowing what you're all about, frees up that space for him to simply add to your confidence. Not be the sole source of it.

A point to bear in mind, is that being eager to please can be seen as being fake because you're always bowing to what others expect. You'll never be seen as authentic. People who aren't honest and clear with what they want can be seen as having a hidden agenda, as people won't know what you stand for. This causes others to back away from you and your relationships can suffer. Even though your intention is likely to be based on the motto, 'I just want to everyone to be happy' it can come across entirely differently to others. When people are constantly submitting to the will of others at the expense of their own, they can end up being resentful or miserable if they continue this behaviour. This is due to constantly trying to fit in with everyone, to have everyone like you so everybody is happy. Everyone that is except you. When you find that all that time you spent trying to please everyone and fit in has been wasted, that's when those feelings of resentment can fester. Realising not everyone likes you is hard to accept when you don't know who you are or what you're about.

Let me share something a client wrote about on this topic:

"At high school there was the in-crowd like any other school and I was so eager to fit in with them that I was willing to do almost anything. Not that they had any particular set of rules or expectations around doing stuff to be one of them, it wasn't like that. They were the popular kids – the ones who looked good, were good at sport and everybody seemed to like. I wanted to be just like them.

In the year that followed, I had worked my way to being almost classed as being one of them. What I found myself doing without even realising it was agreeing with the consensus of the group about things, not having my own opinion, running around making sure their lives were better – at the cost to myself. I would be spending time with one of the girls who was popular, gossiping about others to seem cool, doing her hair before school and was constantly busy doing stuff for her as well as the group. I had little time left for myself.

By the time I left school I was confused, angry, hurt and even a little resentful. I didn't know who I was anymore. I was so keen to fit in with the popular crowd, that I had lost myself in the process. By the age of nineteen, I was on anti-depressants, sad and miserable with no clue who I was anymore. I had been so eager to please everyone, to make sure everyone was happy, that I forgot to do the same for myself.

I couldn't say no, I didn't want to be mean and I was too scared I'd lose them if I did. I didn't want to let anyone down either. By the time I was in my forties, I was so used to doing everything for everyone else, I had no time left for me. I mean, what's the worst that could have happened? They'd give me an odd look, perhaps question me, big deal. But I thought I couldn't say no! I couldn't let them all down.

I was so confused and I had no clue what to do next. I was left empty, bitter and knew something had to change. I was desperately unhappy and my confidence was in the toilet."

When the light of realisation occurs and we acknowledge that we need to put ourselves first, the doors of possibilities open up. Exploring options and having fun trying out new ideas is all part of the journey of self-discovery. People who know what they want and do what it takes to have it, have more to give others as a result. Getting coached to create sustainable change was the move my client obviously chose. She chose to put herself first, she chose to seek assistance and she learned and improved her life because she did. She learned to say no and found her confidence by committing to the process. She no longer sacrifices herself or her happiness. She's learned to be a healthy selfish.

Taking care of ourselves from a holistic point of view, forms the basis of living a functional and healthy life. If you're not sleeping well, if you're not eating a well-balanced diet and not exercising, it affects your physical and mental wellbeing. If you aren't taking proper care of your own needs first, how are you going to help anyone else? An engine that runs at sixty percent capacity compared to an engine that runs at full speed will reap completely different results. The same applies to us. We need to prioritise ourselves – our health, our sleeping habits, our mental wellbeing if we want to help others. We need to be running at one hundred percent capacity each day and not at sixty.

Struggles and challenges are a fact of life. Some are caused from not saying yes to yourself because of wanting to fit in with the crowd and meet the expectations of others. To make everyone feel comfortable. Ask yourself, do you hang around with people who only fit in and don't have an opinion on things? Or with people who enjoy doing different things, exploring life and having adventures? Are you drawn to those who know exactly what they want? What sort of people do you hang around? If you aren't entirely happy with it, then it's time to do something about it and put yourself first.

If you're hanging out with people who lack direction and who aren't stimulating to be around you need to get more selfish. If you don't change the people you hang out with, you'll continue to be surrounded by others who hold you back. You'll continue to not have a voice, to people-please and keep the peace for peace sake and one day look back on life with regret. Developing a healthy attitude, healthy selfishness – putting self first, helps a person to not only grow internally, but outwardly people will begin to be drawn to the new you. You in turn, will be drawn to those who challenge you and help you grow and the negative people in your life will begin to drop off.

Selfishness in this context is not getting your way on everything or ignoring the needs of others. It's not about pleasing yourself at the expense of others. It's about pursuing what's important to you, even if it risks others questioning you and trying to undermine your pursuit. It's about you being intrinsically happy. Your happiness is not contingent upon whether others approve or not, it's whether you have satisfied yourself. This can only be achieved when you start putting you first.

Questions to ask yourself:

1. Are you over obliging? When was the last time you said no to someone?

2. Can you commit to doing something selfish every day? If yes, journal any changes you experience as a result. Could you then sustain this for longer?

3. What have you learned about putting yourself first?

It's time to start scheduling in activities that aid your personal growth and development and plan for the future. You now have tools in your belt to help you deal with people who don't agree with your choices, to let go of people in your circle that aren't helping you achieve personal success and allow like-minded positive people to replace them.

Tool 9

The blame game and fear

"Don't let the fear of what could happen make nothing happen."
Doe Zantamata

A real or a perceived fear can be terrifying and not being able to distinguish between the two can be even more crippling. However, when it comes to self-improvement, we need to learn to use the tools within us to deal with unfamiliar or 'scary' situations and create new associations to overcome perceived fears. We all have these tools innately, but sometimes we need to pull out the sharpener and sharpen the blade of self-belief and tool up with new learnings to cut through those barriers.

Fear can manifest itself in various ways, however, fear can boil down to a handful of areas. People get concerned with the potential to fail and end up settling for a life that they hadn't planned for. The fear of failing becomes so great, that it cripples their goals and dreams which dictates their actions. They become prisoners to the fear they've subconsciously manifested and therefore don't end up trying to achieve them anymore.

Another subconscious fear we can create is having our hearts broken and fear being loved. This can manifest itself in self-sabotaging behaviours to protect ourselves. Past relationships where individuals have experienced heartbreak can set the tone for future relationships. We all want acceptance and love that's unconditional, but when our hearts have been broken and we have experienced rejection, it becomes challenging to allow others back in. The fear once again determines what type of future we create for ourselves. If we let it.

When we think about achieving a goal, more often than not the what ifs pop up creating unnecessary anguish and anxiety even. What if I fail? What if it doesn't work out? What if I'm no good? What if no-one likes it? What if, what if, what if. When we allow the roller coaster of thinking about scenarios that haven't even happened yet to get away from us, we end up spending our time worrying about things that haven't even occurred or possibly may never occur.

The irony is, if we stopped worrying and started redirecting our thinking patterns towards achieving goals we wanted, not only would we be creating a better future for ourselves, but the stress and worry would be alleviated as well. We wouldn't spend time focused on being too scared to try, thinking about all the possible scenarios of how things could go wrong and won't work out, but instead we'd spend time doing the work necessary to achieve goals. By putting plans into action and using our time more effectively, we stop worrying about the possibilities of things going wrong and start focusing our energy on how things can go right.

Some of the classic statements people use are: 'It's just not the right time yet', 'I'm too busy to…', 'When I feel up to it, I'll do it', 'I just don't have the time', 'I'll do it later.' Procrastination seems to sit down and get comfortable with us, which is a form of fear and laziness in disguise. It's when we become slaves to putting things off and allow procrastination to dictate our thoughts and actions, that a problem begins manifesting into something larger. It takes over if we aren't careful. We use the excuse that it isn't the right time, but the reality is, there is no right time. We don't realise we use these as excuses and justifications as to why we aren't acting. If we don't act, nothing changes. If nothing changes, we are perpetually stuck. The more we use delaying tactics to act because of excuses and fear, the harder it becomes to do anything until we stop believing we can ever achieve it. All of this then leads to a decreased sense of self-worth and lowered self-esteem. If the cycle continues it can not only lead to the victim mentality, but to serious psychological disorders such as depression and anxiety. The good news is it doesn't have to.

Fear doesn't go away by waiting for it to pass or hoping and wishing it will either. We use the excuse that it isn't the right time because we are too frightened to act. We procrastinate, finding any reason we can that seems reasonable enough to believe, to avoid doing the thing we're afraid to do. We put things off using delaying tactics, finding other things to do that seem reasonable enough, but aren't really the priority in that moment. We tell ourselves we are just so busy, we just didn't have the time and now it's too late to do anything about it. Story after story to make it okay to ourselves, until even we get sick of hearing the stories we use to justify our lack of commitment.

When I hear clients say things like 'I'm going to when…' or 'I might', what they're really saying is, they won't do it. The lack of commitment in the choice of wording is a reflection of symptomatic patterns of being caught in the web of fear. These statements mean nothing and are just a polite way of saying, 'No, I choose not to' or 'I really can't be bothered'. Again, some might retort with, 'I didn't have a choice' or 'I just couldn't do it', which again is saying, 'In this moment, I choose not to act.' Choosing not to act doesn't break the cycle of fear, it doesn't put a spoke in the wheel to stop it turning – it only keeps the cycle of fear moving.

What a lot of people don't realise, is that being fearful is a choice. Choosing not to act will only make the fear grow and undoubtedly the psychological and physiological symptoms will worsen. We can continue to choose to be scared, continue to use excuses or we can simply say yes to ourselves and be courageous. What's the worst that can happen? Using decisive language, choosing to commit to a decision you've made and then acting on it, consistently opens the door for you to feel courage. We need to learn to face the task that we *think* causes the fear and do it anyway. Courage is achieved this way and courage is not needed when sitting on the couch watching television feeling sorry for yourself. If you want to feel braver, if you want to conquer fear, then start by getting off the couch and doing the thing you *think* you're afraid of. With fear and courage, it is an either/ or situation – you can't have both. If you want to build your confidence and experience courage, start by taking decisive action.

If you think about your biggest goal you want to achieve that you haven't accomplished yet, if you're like most people the answer is probably due to fear. You may not even realise it is due to fear, but it is. We are fearful of change. We're focused on being too scared, too worried about the what if scenarios, choosing to play those out in our mind, instead of devoting that energy to meaningful action. This makes fear continue to grow until it becomes our focus. It becomes all we think about, thereby eliminating the possibility for optimism and positive thinking when we need it most. What if I have a panic attack? What if it doesn't work out? What will people think if I fail? The self-perpetuating cycle of doubt, unnecessary worry and ultimately fear, continues because *that* is the focus to the exclusion of all else.

Fear is the limiting factor stopping you from working towards what you really want. Fear is cunning in its approach; it wears all sorts of disguises and leads to excuses and justifications, but it doesn't have to. Learning how to overcome perceived fear is one of the most liberating pursuits you can undertake. You can learn to harness it for good.

It's easy to pretend or to not acknowledge that fear isn't the major influencer when we don't achieve what we set out to. We then set a path in motion, whereby we lay the foundations to not achieving success, by laying brick after brick of excuses. We tell ourselves stories of why we can't achieve something, how badly the odds are stacked against us in achieving and get so caught up in the reasons why not to achieve, that there isn't any room to do the thing anyway. Instead of using fear as a reason why not to achieve, fear can be used as a motivator.

If you let fear chase you away from achieving, then you've effectively given in. You've told yourself so many stories about why you can't achieve, that you've now got yourself caught up in the self-pity trap. People who get caught up in this cycle have thousands of reasons why they haven't achieved personal and/or professional success. They'll be happy to tell you all their reasons why they haven't achieved if you'd allow them to. They feel victimised, that they've been given a raw deal in life, that it was a series of bad luck that stopped them and so on. Again, story after story to tell themselves and others to justify their lack of integrity and motivation towards success.

It takes courage to act, it takes courage to do something to get out of the situation you're in, but it doesn't take any courage to sit back and feel sorry for yourself. Sitting back and doing nothing to help yourself only helps justify the excuses you have and you end up missing opportunities to develop yourself further. Without me telling you how it is and challenging that comfortability, positive change may elude you. Sometimes it takes someone else to help you wake up to the fact that you're wasting your gifts and talents. Perhaps you feel as though you don't have any or that you're not that good at anything. Is that really true? Are you telling yourself more stories, more justifications that make it okay to stay the same? How long could you really tolerate living with these excuses eating away at your conscience before you decide to act? Justifications we tell ourselves are what makes it difficult to ever really see things improving and so people who live like this, end up living mediocre lives and aren't willing to challenge the status quo. They're too comfortable where they're at.

Fear is an instinct we all share and can be used to one's advantage if a person knows how. Harnessing that instinct to use to our advantage can be the single greatest motivator that propels us forward towards success. Nothing would seem too difficult, too deterring or off-putting and any obstacles would then be viewed as mere bumps in the road. Every genuinely successful person on the planet has attained their success by working hard to achieve it. That's a given, we expect that. What we don't often realise, is that they too encountered many obstacles and had to deal with fear at every turn.

People like Oprah Winfrey, who was one of my favourite role models, encountered many obstacles along the road of success. Oprah would share her struggles and triumphs with her audience members and how she was able to overcome fear, to become one of the world's greatest success stories. I'm certainly not saying that we have to aim as high as people like her, what I am saying is, people like Oprah have used models of excellence and multiple strategies to overcome fear they encountered. They smashed the boundaries of fear at every turn and became role models to inspire many to bettering themselves.

Initially, when we encounter fear the mind begins to worry. It worries about the financial costs, the ifs and buts, the real and the perceived. But the questions that are worth thinking about are not those focused on the imagined – on situations that haven't even occurred or may never occur. What can really be achieved if we are constantly worrying? How can we achieve personal success if our focus is consumed with possible scenarios that may never play out? How can we be productive if our energy is being consumed by negative thoughts and being bound by fear? How much self-inflicted psychological pain are we willing to tolerate at the expense of pleasure, before we decide enough is enough?

These types of questions are sometimes difficult to hear, particularly the issue around taking responsibility for ourselves. It can appear to some that when we talk about responsibility, we are somehow implying that everyone who is experiencing fear is automatically lacking the maturity to handle it. That's not it at all. Let me illustrate my point with some examples, to show you how a lack of responsibility for the way we respond to things, can lead to the victim mentality and a feeling of being powerless. When we feel powerless, we feel we don't have choices and are a victim in the circumstances that are happening. We feel a lack of control. If we don't address the issue of not taking responsibility, of not developing the confidence to have a voice, then the cycle of victimisation and self-destructive negative self-talk continues. The joy of life, the very essence of experiencing love and satisfaction, get sucked out of every situation we have, unless we can place a spoke in the wheel and stop the cycle from turning.

Case study one:

Jim is an executive who lives in a constant state of anxiety. He says that the people around him are causing him stress and that they need to change. If they did, then everything would be fine. If only his wife was more understanding that he has to work the hours he does, if only the president of the company would stop pressuring him for deadlines, if only his son would stop drinking, then he would be fine. If only, if only, if only. He doesn't believe that there is any reason for him to get help, the issue lies with everyone else. It's all their fault.

What Jim doesn't understand, is that he isn't taking responsibility for how he is responding to the experiences he is having. He believes the issue is with everyone else and that he is the victim in every situation he is involved in. What he doesn't realise, is that he has the power to choose how he responds to each of these situations, that the power to change how he feels about them all lies with him. He just hasn't figured that out yet. He hasn't taken responsibility for the decisions he is currently making and feels powerless to change how they affect him.

Case study two:

Maree feels like life couldn't get any better. She has a great circle of friends, a wonderful job and is happy with her current partner. Her continual complaints are about her ex-husband who she says is making her life miserable. She says that he never supports her, has always been unfair to her and doesn't pay child support. On top of that, she says her teenage son is turning against her and tells her that she is being selfish. She says she is feeling so tired all of the time and that her energy levels are down and blames her ex-husband and son's actions for the way she feels.

Like Jim, Maree is not taking responsibility for how she is choosing to experience her life. Her constant complaints about her ex-husband and how her son is making life so bad for her, dominate her conversations with others. It's all she seems to talk about. Maree has chosen to focus on two small aspects of her life, that for her are a major issue. The problem is, her focus is at the exclusion of all else. She's forgotten that she has a wonderful circle of friends, her dream job and an amazing partner and again falls victim to the circumstances around her, which she has then allowed to determine the level of joy and happiness she experiences – or lack thereof. Her lack of focus on what she *does* have and the focus turned to what she *doesn't* have, has manifested itself physically and psychologically to the detriment of her wellbeing. Maree needs to take responsibility for her life, responsibility for the choices she makes and the conversations she has with others, if she wants things to improve. She can determine the reality she wants to experience, but it starts with changing her focus and what she talks about with others.

The issue for many divorced people or singles who have separated from partners, is that they continually talk negatively about them. They talk about how lonely they are, how bad their boss is at work, how difficult it is to find a partner these days and so on. That's not to say that people who are married don't complain either. Many complain about their spouse, about how their children haven't followed in their footsteps, that there is never enough money, that they never get to go on the holidays they want, the lack of effective communication they experience with their spouse and so on. Again it illustrates my point about responsibility. None of these people who choose to focus on the issues, to constantly complain about how bad things are, how tough the economy is right now and how others just keep letting them down, are taking responsibility for how they are experiencing life. As a result of this, it then determines the level of happiness they experience and they become less than successful role models for others. People remember the gist of conversations of what you chose to talk about and if you continually focused on the negative aspects, it then shapes how people view you in return.

It pays to mention here that issues like the economy, those things that we don't have control over and aren't in a position to change, don't warrant our attention to the degree of constantly whinging about it. What purpose does it serve? If we are constantly complaining about how life sucks, that we don't have this and don't have that and continually focus on things out of our realm of influence, what purpose does it have in helping ourselves live a better life and feeling confident?

People who have these types of conversations that dominate the content with which they converse, is a reflection of the level of satisfaction they're experiencing in their own lives. It's similar to when people gossip. The venom that sprouts forth out of their mouths about other people, is a real indicator of what *they* feel inside and that ugliness is sprouted forth verbally. This outward display of negativity and little to no self-respect, is not what we want to surround ourselves with when we are trying to improve. However, the point is, people who have frivolous conversations and who don't challenge themselves, are trapped by fear in one way or another. They are not role models for courage and excellence, but are role models for negativity and being bound by fear.

The blame game involves aspects like – blaming others, blaming our environment, blaming whatever. It allows us to shift the responsibility onto someone or something else and therefore we play the victim. 'If this didn't happen, or that didn't happen, or if she would stop doing such and such, then everything would be fine,' are the type of conversation starters that can be used when we're in the victim mentality. When we're in the victim mentality, we show a lack of maturity because the blame gets shifted elsewhere. Fear is now manifesting itself into a cycle of self-pity, which allows us to feel comfortable and be complacent. We have allowed the fear to control our lives instead of harnessing its power for good.

Fear of failure, fear of rejection, fear that we're just not good enough are typical of the types of fears people have. Fear is a natural current that runs through all of our veins. If we let it, fear can dominate and control and keep us locked up in the prison of comfortability and complacency. Being challenged is out of the question right now. It's this living in fear that causes a conundrum; we're unfulfilled and feeling dissatisfied with life, unhappy with the status quo of things, yet at the same time too afraid to pursue anything better 'in case it doesn't work out'.

If we allow it, fear can control our lives, dictate our actions and all without us noticing it. So why is it we put up with living in fear? To understand the underlying psychology so that you can actively work against its control is important. To a point, fear and anxiety have a place in a healthy human's psyche. Fear is a normal emotion, triggered by a real or perceived threat to our existence that we all instinctively have. It helped man survive when they had to hunt for food, but the problem is, we aren't having to go out hunting anymore. If we don't retrain our mind and tame the instinct of reacting to fear, then it can become hypersensitive and develop into conditions such as anxiety. Statistics tell us that one in five people have experienced anxiety of some description, with half of those people experiencing debilitating symptoms.

Everything from lifestyle choices, social media, caffeine usage and so on have been blamed for our current state of anxiety. Living in a state of blame again shifts the responsibility onto something else, that it is something else's fault that has made us feel this way. Averting the responsibility outwardly this way, doesn't allow us to solve the issue, because the blame is now 'out there' and therefore, there's nothing that can be done about it, but just live with it. It reinforces that victim mentality, where we fall prey to circumstances and believe wholeheartedly that the issue doesn't lie with us at all. However, living in a state of blame has never helped anyone solve their problems – it's only added to them. As a result of these issues left to their own devices, many have been given quick fixes such as prescription medication to cope with the symptoms of anxiety, rather than tackling the very issues that caused it in the first place. It's time to take ownership of our feelings and learn how to stop living in fear. We need to re-educate ourselves and learn new and better ways that actually help us live a happier life, rather than reaching for a bottle of Valium to stop the symptoms.

It's an unfortunate reality today that people want the quick fixes and aren't willing to invest in programs that can give them long-term solutions. Taking medication may help with the symptoms of anxiety, but it certainly doesn't tackle the underlying issue and get to the heart of the matter. If we aren't willing to put ourselves first and realise we are worth so much more than what we are currently settling for, nothing will change. The same old habits will play out, the same old routines, the same old feelings of dissatisfaction will linger, bubbling away beneath the surface. If we do this long enough, just like a shaken bottle of champagne pops – so will we. If we don't start addressing the deep-seated issues and find out what is holding us back, we will continue to be trapped by fear and its symptoms will only worsen with time. We need to find a remedy that works.

Tool 10

Stopping the merry-go-round

"If you want your life to change, your choices must change and today is the best day of your life to begin."

Author unknown

Unfortunately, when we are on that merry-go-round of feeling stuck and of not knowing what to do, the wheels of fear and not feeling that great about ourselves keep turning. We need to learn how to stop feeling fearful and trapped by negative self-talk and doubt and help ourselves not only psychologically, but physically as well. Otherwise, the cycle of fear continues to go unchecked.

Feeling fearful about change has physical ramifications as well and the cause of these symptoms have begun in our minds – the way we are choosing to view things. If we choose to view things through the lens of fear, our actions will be limited and bound by it. If we view things this way, continually creating a habit of limitation, the results we end up with will be sporadic and inconsistent. We don't yet have a clear direction forward with what we want to achieve in life, because the cycle of fear and negativity keeps us going around in circles. We need to tool up and learn how to stop fear from dominating our actions to the detriment of ourselves and achieving purpose and meaning in life, so we have that way forward. When we have a clear and direct path in life, the actions we then take are easy and straight forward. Being bound by fear keeps us trapped and every action we take therefore, feels like a monumental effort. When things feel this way we tend to give up, stop trying and wonder what's the point anyway. It's just too hard.

Because we are naturally lazy, we want things as simple and as easy as possible. When we start associating fear with change, the likelihood of us proactively changing is minimal. We inadvertently create this invisible wall of fear, creating a barrier between achieving success and keeping us stuck where we're at. We are fearful of acting, fearful of the unknown. We have now associated so much pain around changing, that we stay comfortable with the habits of procrastination again and don't act. We have now created such a huge imagery of fear in our minds that we get too afraid to do anything. Fear has gripped us, entangled us in its web and got us right where it wants us – miserable, defeated and unhappy.

So the way we choose to view things has powerful ramifications. If we continue to view change and fear together, we will continue to associate pain with it. The thought of something causing us pain stops us. Indecisiveness and lack of commitment are symptomatic of someone wanting something better, but not knowing how to achieve it yet. We appear to be busy, play games, watch movies, doing whatever it takes to keep us distracted from the unresolved issues deep down. Deep down we know we want more, that we are worthy of more, we're just too scared to admit it and do what it takes to get it. Not knowing how to create a better life for ourselves can make us feel sad, defeated and worthless. We start believing that things will never change for the better. We find ourselves in a world of pain that mindless video games keep us temporarily distracted from. The point to remember is, if you did know how to create that life, you'd be living it right now. Don't let not knowing be a reason to beat yourself up again. That's a cop out.

We typically see pain as being outside of ourselves and comfort close to us. Even if we don't feel that happy with our lives right now, we tend to settle for the way things are. We believe that even when we aren't content, we have to settle for a life that's less than exciting and stimulating, because we haven't learned how to create more happiness for ourselves. We've naturally associated happiness and contentment inside our comfort zone

– even if it is only a marginal amount. We have settled and sold ourselves short of our true potential. Even if life is dishing up a plate of misery right now, the fear around changing is keeping us bound right where we are and it seems way more frightening, than the predicament we're in right now. On top of that, the what if scenarios play out in our minds, keeping us trapped even more out of fear of making a colossal error in judgement. What if I stuff up? What if it doesn't work out? What if…

What if for argument's sake we viewed things differently? What if we were to flip that thinking on its head and alter how we viewed happiness and change? What if instead of focusing on how things can go wrong, we start focusing on how things can go right? That by changing our circumstances we will experience greater satisfaction and happiness. If we do this, we can create a new and positive association around change and wipe away the fear we had formally associated with change. By focusing on happiness and change together, we create a new imagery of an exciting and self-satisfying life outside of our comfort zone. What a dramatic difference that would have on how we viewed things and the actions we would take to change things for ourselves!

With that newly formed association we have created around achieving greater personal success *outside* our comfort zone, we can now focus on *that* instead. Instead of focusing on ways to stop feeling miserable, ticked off and procrastinating, we can formulate a plan forward that is exciting and stimulating. Instead of spending time distracting ourselves mindlessly, we can focus on experiencing more happiness and satisfaction outside our comfort zone. Focusing on the end goal, determines what steps we take to attain it. Breaking it up into smaller, manageable steps to get that goal is where we begin. Letting go of the impatience to have it all sorted straight away, we can then take a step at a time towards achieving our goals. A great acronym to use to help you achieve future success is SMART goals. It stands for – Specific, Measurable, Attainable, Realistic, Timely. It can be used to guide your goal setting so your efforts become targeted and meaningful to break the cycle of fear. Life as it once was, has cost us far too much already and it is time to move forward. Enough is enough.

For example, if you were stuck in a job you didn't get any enjoyment out of, it would make perfect sense to want a different career. Considering the fact we spend the vast majority of our lives working, it would be logical to conclude that the only way to experience greater internal satisfaction, would be to do a job we enjoy doing. To experience more pleasure at work therefore, we would need to move past the fear-based rhetorical questions we create in our minds like – what if it doesn't work out? What if I'm no good at it? What if I make a mistake? Instead of focusing on the possibilities of how things could go wrong, focus on the possibilities of how amazing and exciting life could be. Start getting excited at the prospect of being in a career that you'll love as opposed to one you don't. Instead of trying to manifest something that hasn't even happened, focus on manifesting something positive and truly satisfying instead. This will then determine the actions to take towards achieving your long term goal. Again, use the SMART goal acronym for specific, measurable and timely goal setting, so you hold yourself accountable to achieving future success.

If the dream job entails furthering your education or upskilling to improve performance, it would make sense to do what it takes to get it. By chasing new and improved career options, with careful planning and preparation, it is an immediate way to stop negative thoughts that want to shift the focus back to where you were. By focusing on how enjoyable life will be, as opposed to how bad things are now, it allows the cycle of fear to be broken by taking decisive action that moves you forward, instead of holding you back. You'll be starving negativity and putting it back where it belongs – silent and defeated.

By spending time worrying about something that may not even occur, by manifesting something that hasn't even happened, we can start telling ourselves reasons why we shouldn't or 'can't' make changes. This is a classic example of fear dominating and ruling the decision making process, to the detriment of self and not living up to our mission in life, which ultimately costs us happiness. All because we decided to settle, we decided to let fear rule the day and decide our fate in a thankless and meaningless job. What an unnecessary waste and an unsatisfying way to live life. Instead of getting caught up in this cycle, remind yourself again – what's the worst that can happen? Why is this so important to me? If you're really uncertain and unsure about the changes, create a list of pros and cons and you'll see how making the changes will be the best course of action to take. After all, you want more satisfaction, happiness and internal peace don't you?

The trap of procrastinating, the trap of fear, is that we see it being harder than it really is. I know I've caught myself saying, 'it's too hard, I don't want to' when it came to bettering myself, but when I turned around how I viewed things, I began to feel more courageous and optimistic about creating a better life for myself. I was making excuses for not living up to my potential, because I was allowing fear to take over and feeling scared of change. It's in this instance that the statement, 'feel the fear and do it anyway' does apply. It takes courage to want to be better, but it takes more courage to actually *do* something about it. For to do nothing is action too. It's a conscious decision to stay comfortable, whether we're aware of it or not.

Change and fear can be interwoven and the two concepts get jumbled up together. When this happens our map of the world becomes fear-based. As a result, we stay the same. We're too frightened of change, too scared of taking a risk and scared of the possibility of making a mistake. This is a symptom of a fear-based map; too frightened to have a go, too scared of uncertainty. The more we hang onto the need to keep things as they are the more we stay stuck. Just like the example earlier about the job, we continue to settle and remain unfulfilled and as a result we stagnate. When we see the possibilities as being 'out there', outside of our comfort zone, the likelihood of change is low without a clear plan. That's why getting specific about how much you're suffering right now is so important. It helps you understand that to achieve more pleasure and happiness, you need to see that outside your comfort zone. When we do that, we do what it takes to experience more of it.

Client 'X'

"I'm a Mum of three grown boys who still live with me and am feeling stuck and unsure what to do with my life. I want things to be different but I'm scared of change. I want to be happy. I don't know what to do with my time though. I usually spend time on Facebook or just relaxing each day so I don't really have time to do much else.

The house is a mess, it's getting me down and the boys don't help. I mean they should because they are all grown up, but I don't mind cooking and cleaning for them. After all, I am their Mum. I wanted more for myself now they're grown, but at least I get to spend time with them, I guess that's better than nothing. I should be happy with how life is. I dunno what to do anymore."

If we continue to focus on how we can't change, then we miss opportunities to better ourselves. We settle. We let fear take over and become complacent once more. By focusing on why you want to change and developing a proactive plan of targeted action, this will keep that momentum for change going. Even if it is a little uncomfortable at first, keep reminding yourself it doesn't last. When in the midst of fog, there's always the clearing at the other side. Keeping focused on the clearing ahead, will help keep you moving forward step by step.

However, if we don't have a clear direction of where we want to head in life, then the results will be all over the place. If we don't have a clear goal in mind, a plan in place and the specific actions required to achieve it, then the goal won't be achieved. Even when we do achieve something, it won't be at the level of satisfaction we desire, because we haven't worked out why it's so important to us. It becomes meaningless and not fulfilling. Having a clear path forward, with the steps needed to achieve success is the way to attain that internal peace and satisfaction. If you're feeling like you're still in fog – get a coach.

To illustrate my point, I'll use grocery shopping as the example. When we go shopping with a shopping list, we are less likely to wander from the list and collect items that we don't need. If we do, we tend to tell ourselves things like 'I'll get this just in case', 'I may need this', 'It's on special, so I better get it now' that justify our collection of non-essentials. We have deviated from the plan – deviated from the list and as a result have ended up with a tonne of items we don't need or are unlikely to end up using. The items we don't use, end up sitting on the shelf and by the time we get around to checking the use-by date, it has expired. It was a waste of time and effort getting the extra items and our hip pocket took a battering as well.

Whereas, if we had have stuck to the plan of getting the items on the list, we would have had a clear direction on where we wanted to go in the supermarket and would have saved ourselves time, effort and money buying only the items we needed. The cupboard wouldn't be cluttered with unnecessary junk, we wouldn't have wasted food and we'd feel good about ourselves that we stuck to the list – stuck to the plan. When I've gone grocery shopping when I'm hungry, I have walked out with so many unnecessary extras that later I felt guilty about. This then became the catalyst to beat myself for being wasteful, for the 'I should've known better' sentiment and the negative self-talk started again. All because I didn't stick to a plan and I allowed the hunger pangs to dictate my actions. Just like hunger pangs dictated my actions, so too can self-doubt and negativity determine what meaningful actions we take – or don't for that matter.

If we are moving towards a new specific aim, there will be meaningful and decisive action in it. Having a reason why we want to change, why we want to push through the boundaries of fear is crucial. When we have our eyes on the prize, have a clear cut target to focus on, we are more energetic and determined to achieve the goal in mind. When N.A.S.A. decided they wanted to send a man into space and go to the moon, they didn't project him into the atmosphere without a clear idea of where they wanted to go. They had planned and prepared for the mission for years. Admittedly, it took many failed attempts, but they eventually reached their goal of landing a man on the moon. They took those previous failed attempts and learned from them. They re-assessed their plans and all aspects of the mission. Beating the Soviets in sending man into space before the end of the decade, was the all-important reason to achieve their goal – and they did.

Having that compelling reason why change is important is critical to achieving the results we seek. I'll use the example of losing weight. If we don't have a clearly defined goal why losing weight is so important, the effort necessary to achieve weight loss will be inconsistent. The scales will waver, the calorie intake will differ and the exercise plan will be erratic. Any time a hiccup occurs, when the effort of losing weight is not being reflected on the scales, the weight loss goal can become shaky. It's at these stages that the cracks start to appear and the snares of negativity start to filter through and we begin to question our commitment. We can fall back into the trap of telling ourselves we can't do it and it's too hard. Justifications like, 'well, at least I tried' making it okay to fail and lowering our expectations with each statement. We excuse poor performance levels. That's not okay.

It could easily be solved by working out why the weight loss was important in the first place. Having a clearly defined goal of *why* weight loss is important, would allow the actions we take to be clearly defined, a set plan in place with details about eating habits, calorie intake and an exercise regime all set-out and planned daily. All towards a clearly defined goal. When the hiccups do come, we have a clear plan and our reason for losing the weight to fall back on. It becomes the priority and focus, not fear anymore.

If you decide to use this tool to achieve the dream job, to lose weight or to make some other significant change in your life, it's important to stack the pain of how bad things are currently, so your mind grasps the concept that more pleasurable experiences are outside your comfort zone. Once you understand these concepts and apply them in an area of life you are wanting to create positive change around, you'll start to see results. It takes commitment, making errors and learning from those mistakes, so the actions you take are decisive, meaningful and sustainable. This way the decisions you make have a lasting impact, but it starts with how you view things. How you now see fear and whether you turn it into a positive and harness it for actionable change is up to you. Fear doesn't have to cripple us, it can help focus and drive us forward.

A few points to remember about this area on fear; it shouldn't be seen as a bad thing that must be avoided at all costs – not at all. Fear is an instinct we all have, but when it comes to transforming our lives, having a fear-based map and living in fear, being trapped by negative thoughts and emotions and lacking in self-worth is not a way to live life. There are far too many things we miss out on if we view everything in life from a fear-based point of view. Fear has its place in our lives, but it's knowing how to harness it and use it to propel you forward that is the key.

To change that fear-based map, to ultimately turn things around for ourselves, we need to start believing in ourselves and developing a can-do attitude. When we start viewing mistakes as errors instead of failures, when we see errors as learning curves, it helps develop a positive mindset. We are going to make errors – that's guaranteed. The key is they only become mistakes if we continually repeat the same thing over and over and don't learn from them. If, however, we give ourselves permission to make errors, then we don't have any reason to beat ourselves up for making mistakes or failing. If we don't break the cycle of negative self-talk, we end up down the road of self-pity and justifications again, telling ourselves it's okay to fail and stories like 'it's just not meant to be'. That damages a person's level of confidence and their self-esteem and we once again settle for a life that's less than fulfilling.

Just remember, if it isn't serving you, it's harming you and therefore, you need to let it go. It doesn't have a place in your life as it serves no purpose but to harm. Viewing things positively and optimistically is a way to overcome fear and harness its elements for good. We all need to put a spoke in the wheel of negative self-talk and adopt a can-do attitude instead. You can do it, you just have to start believing you can and you will overcome fear to live a happier life instead. You can stop the merry-go-round of negativity and you can start by getting on the empowerment ride instead.

Tool 11

$\smile$

The Gr rule

"Without gratitude, life can be lonely, depressing and impoverished. Gratitude enriches human life. It elevates, energizes, inspires and transforms, and those who practice it will experience significant improvements in several areas of life including relationships, academics, energy level and even dealing with tragedy and crisis."
Dr Robert Emmons, Professor of Psychology, University of California.

Dr Emmons states, "Despite all of the scientific evidence and research that demonstrates the ability of gratitude to impact positive change to mood, motivation and mindset, the daily practice of gratitude is not a widely adopted habit within our 'quick fix, instant gratification' society." I couldn't agree more. What we see on television screens are advertisements that appeal to our desire for greed. 'But wait there's more' is a term that's often used when selling a product, that if you buy it you will also receive something else as an extra, to reel you in to instantly satisfy the desire for more. It appeals to us because just like shopping in the supermarket without a list, we tend to buy extra things 'just in case', or better yet, because it's on special. It somehow justifies spending extra because you ultimately get more. It instantly gratifies and it satisfies the desire for greed. What we feed by buying into this type of behaviour is our desire for more and we feed that instead. Being grateful and content has eluded us.

Gratitude, like cognitive behavioural therapy, has become increasingly popular in recent years and the benefits of its practice are regularly written about in a variety of mainstream magazines and blogs, by specialist health professionals such as psychologists. Forbes magazine published an article titled, *Seven Scientifically Proven Benefits of Gratitude That Will Motivate You to Give Thanks Year-Round*. The article listed the following benefits:

- Gratitude opens the door to more relationships
- Gratitude improves physical health
- Gratitude improves psychological health
- Gratitude improves empathy and reduces aggression
- Grateful people sleep better
- Gratitude improves self-esteem
- Gratitude increases mental strength

I came up with the 'Gr rule' one day when journaling and thought it was easy and simple enough for anyone to start implementing in their lives too. The Gr rule as defined by me is, *'what we take for granted is what we need to be grateful for'*. As obvious as it may sound, we often forget to be grateful for the things we *do* have, as opposed to what we *don't* have and therefore, we limit our focus. Unfortunately, gratitude is one of the least likely of all resources to be implemented by people and yet it is the easiest one to do. Perhaps therein lies the problem; people think just because it is simple and easy, that it is too good to be true and therefore, don't give it a go. However, once you master the geniality behind using this tool, you'll understand it's powerful enough to help improve your life.

If you think of the torch example I gave earlier in the book and the light that torch beams out, the lit area becomes the light of gratitude. What you place inside that lit area then becomes your focus to the exclusion of all else. Everything outside of the torch's beam is in darkness and has now been excluded from the light and the more you place inside the light – the greater the light grows.

If you picture yourself picking up more and more things to be grateful for and placing them in the front of the torch, the amount of things that light focuses on grows until there is little darkness left. The light is so strong, there is so much gratitude there, that even in the darkest of times, you've put so many things into the ray of light, that it becomes all-consuming. It is a complete shift of focus from one of ingratitude and taking things for granted, to one of humbleness, gentleness and kindness. By focusing on the light of gratitude, an attitude shift is the result. The desire for more is no longer the determining factor dictating our actions.

That's not to say that everyone who isn't grateful all the time takes everything for granted – not at all. However, I will challenge you by getting you to think about the last time you were genuinely grateful for simple things like the air you breathe or the clothes on your back? When was the last time you were grateful for the home you live in or the food on your table? When we start breaking down these things, when we start analysing just how much there is to be thankful for, how can negativity have room to fester? The two cannot co-exist together in the same space – it is an either-or situation.

I know when I began journaling and started to concentrate my efforts on all the positive things that were happening in my life, it helped shift my focus entirely. That's not to say, I was naive and buried my head in the sand and didn't recognise that many things were happening that could easily have swallowed me up and drowned me in a pool of doom and gloom. A very real example was the worldwide pandemic Covid19, which I'm sure those who read this will well and truly relate to. This was an example of how circumstances which were beyond our control, could quite easily have taken over to become the main point of focus. We could have been consumed with the possible pending effects on our lives and succumbed to a monothematic focus to the exclusion of gratitude and optimism.

Yes, Covid19 impacted us all and for some it meant the loss of income, security and their working lives. It impacted me professionally as well, with most of the courses I usually run having to be cancelled. I also teach a dance class and that too was cancelled. It meant I had to re-adjust things and I had to create a new normal like everyone else, but in doing so, I saw it as an opportunity to learn new skills and to write this book. I saw this pandemic through the eyes of gratitude. I saw it as an opportunity that I normally wouldn't have. I was grateful for the chance.

For some, however, this pandemic was the catalyst for depression, anxiety and feelings of isolation and hopelessness consumed them. When we focus our attention on how bad things could possibly affect us, it can impact us negatively. Focusing our attention on what we *don't* have as opposed to what we *do*, takes away the ability to see events like these as an opportunity to do other things. We weren't told to stay home and not learn, we weren't told to stop talking to one another, we weren't told we couldn't write, draw, sing or create. We didn't have it that bad really, depending on which way we chose to view it. During Covid19, it was a chance for families to re-connect on a deeper level, to play board games, learn cooking techniques, have more meaningful conversations with their children and/or parents. It was an opportunity that wouldn't have been available to families under normal circumstances, to strengthen their relationships with one another. In that sense, Covid19 could be seen through the lens of gratitude and as a bonus for strengthening family ties.

These were the blessings hidden amongst the negativity of the pandemic if we chose to view it that way. They were the things we'd normally take for granted as not being an option to do. Taking those opportunities and choosing to focus on what we have and strengthen the ties of kinship, allowed us to feel more gratitude and appreciation. Moments like these don't come around very often, but when something like this happens, instead of focusing on the negative aspects and allowing it to affect our mental wellbeing, by choosing gratitude, we can reach new levels of self-awareness and appreciation. It widens the torches' beam and places more items in front of the light, which diminishes the capacity of negativity to significantly impact us.

Being grateful in any situation is a reflection of the level of self-awareness a person has. Having an attitude of gratitude doesn't mean you're immune to negativity or are in denial about it either. It's saying that no matter what the situation is that presents itself, there are always options, always alternatives and it's always positive. When we grasp this concept and use this tool regularly, our perspective shifts and we see every moment as an opportunity or a learning curve. It never puts down.

People who can do this become the leaders and role models for others to follow. It's people like these who can stand up and lead. We naturally gravitate towards them and seek their leadership skills in moments of crisis. It's by their example that others are by association, able to be influenced by their incredulous ability to see the good in amongst the bad. It's these people who have been able to successfully transform their lives and are likely to help transform the lives of others in a positive and impactful way. They understand the power behind gratitude and its application into everyday life when practised consistently. It becomes ingrained into the very core of who they are.

That's not to say that we don't deny the realities of situations such as a global pandemic and don't recognise the life-changing impact it can have on our very way of life. It's having the ability to decide how much information we allow to be filtered into our consciousness. It's choosing how much is enough to keep us informed and updated without overwhelming ourselves. It's being able to create that balance, to know when enough is enough and switching the television off and choosing an alternate activity instead. Gratitude has the ability to build awareness and wisdom if we practice it regularly. It becomes automated that in every situation the focus is positive. It becomes effortless.

Because the reality is, if we don't develop this ability and exercise the muscle of positive decision making, then we get sucked into the vacuum of negativity and feel out of control, isolated and even victimised. If we don't practice gratitude, practice being positive and shifting our focus every day, then the vacuum of negativity will suck us into feelings of despair.

Being grateful has a flow-on effect in other areas of our lives too. It helps create a balance to develop a deeper appreciation for things we would normally take for granted. When life returned to 'normal' and we were allowed to re-join our respective workplaces, undoubtedly the number one feeling we experienced was gratitude. We were thankful for things returning back to the way they were. We saw surges in restaurants and cafes and a spike in tourism, because when something is taken away from us and is then returned, it gives us a deeper sense of appreciation for it. This was a great lesson for all of us in not taking anything in life for granted as a given, that we'll automatically have it all, the way we want all the time. That's why implementing the gr rule is so important and powerful, as it's moments like these that make us appreciate things just that little bit more and gives us the ability to see the beauty amongst the chaos and mayhem.

Think of a time when you may have been ill or a loved one was and how that affected you. The heartache, the physical pain and the endurance to overcome it, all of those elements you experienced and the joy and relief you felt when things returned to normal. Those experiences would have undoubtedly developed a deeper sense of appreciation and gratitude for health returning to normal. I can relate to this very well. In one instance in 2018, when I underwent major surgery alone and was under anaesthetic for eight hours, my ability to see the good in things was put to the test as well.

That time for me helped me develop a deeper sense of gratitude. I had a bowel obstruction, twisted bowel, an internal hernia and a mass of adhesions smothering and enveloping what little of my small bowel I had left. I had already endured almost forty surgeries over the years and had lost my large bowel several years earlier and subsequently, had to wear an ileostomy bag for two years. Thankfully that was reversed, however, going into that surgery in 2018, I realised I was in a very precarious state and being alone and away from family, made it even harder.

I remember putting out an appeal via a live video on Facebook from my hospital bed, asking people to pray for me and it went viral. I spoke from the heart, told them what I was facing the following morning and the amount of love and support I received was more than I could have imagined. Lots of comments and likes and shares as well and countless individuals and groups prayed for my safety and wellbeing for the operation.

It was also a test for me personally for my faith in God Himself and realising that it was only Him that could see me through this operation and what I needed was an answer to prayer. I prayed and prayed and had asked others to pray that I didn't get that dreaded bag back. Thankfully I didn't. The surgeons were shocked at the convoluted mess internally and had worked extremely hard to make sure they didn't puncture my bowel. My prayer had been answered. I can remember running my hands over my abdomen and not feeling anything foreign stuck to me and only the smoothness of my skin. It was in that moment, I developed an even greater sense of gratitude than I had ever previously had.

Yes, it took me months and months to recover, but I believe without that attitude of gratitude I had developed and my faith in God Almighty, I don't believe my recovery would have been as good as it was. He was the rope I hung onto through the entire ordeal and I had also prayed that my daughter would somehow be with me. Amazingly, she came! Right towards the end of my hospital stay, when I was battling psychologically, she walked through my hospital room and said, 'Hi Mum.'

I can remember looking up from the chair in the room and seeing this beautiful ray of sunshine walk in with a huge smile on her face, arms outstretched to help me get up to embrace her. It was my precious daughter. I couldn't believe my eyes. She had taken time off work, made arrangements for where she would stay interstate, booked and paid for flights and surprised me at the hospital. I can remember sobbing and sobbing because of the joy and relief I felt upon her embrace. That human contact, that special someone who picks you up when you're so low, the one thing I desperately needed and once again, my prayers had been answered. Once again, I was grateful.

Developing an attitude of gratitude, the gr rule, is a mighty powerful tool. Through the unrelenting pain I felt physically and mentally in hospital, I hung onto that thread of faith and gratitude. I had prayed I wouldn't get an ileostomy bag and I didn't. I was grateful for the love and support I received from others. I was grateful that the pain I had been experiencing before the surgery would be alleviated. I was grateful to the doctors and nurses for the amazing care I received. I was grateful for my daughter's surprise visit right when I needed it. Most of all, I was grateful to God Himself. When we recognise the amazing power of gratitude in our lives and how even in the darkest of times and our most challenging moments, we can still find something to be thankful for, it can transform our lives. If you can find something positive to be thankful for consistently, it shifts the focus from pain and darkness to that of love and light.

If I use the Covid19 experience again, sometimes doing random acts of kindness (or being the recipient of one), can help strengthen that attitude as well. Being kind to others allows positivity to thrive and grow and the light from the torch widens as a result. These seemingly small, selfless deeds done by others can be the one spark that brightens a person's day. I know when the pandemic became the number one talking point, we were bombarded with scenes of people rushing to the supermarket cleaning out the shelves of toilet paper. It became the hot item that no-one could seem to buy. I happened to be the fortunate recipient of a random act of kindness by one of my neighbours, who had decided that if she woke up early the following morning, would buy toilet paper, (if it was available) for our complex.

She did wake up and then proceeded to knock on all our doors later that day and hand out rolls of toilet paper. She asked for nothing in return, she only wanted to help make things easier for us all. This kind gesture brightened all of our days and this random act of kindness allowed gratitude to flourish. She walked away feeling good about herself knowing she had helped and for us it was also a lesson in humility.

Gratitude can affect every aspect of our lives if we allow it to. It is linked with being positive and optimistic regardless of what is happening around us. If you can learn to implement this simple and easy technique in your daily life, practise it consistently, then you are well on your way to transforming your life to being a positive, optimistic and healthier one. Gratitude affects every aspect of a human being's existence and even when things don't seem to be going that well, it can be the one tool you need to help see you through it. Even a smile is showing gratitude.

Having a positive mindset is such an advantage when situations like a global pandemic happen. It's easy to get dragged into the trap that everything is bleak, that there's no hope, but being positive allows the mind to be ironclad strong, to embrace new and exciting ventures like being creative and is the one weapon we can use to deal with these types of situations. Having said all of that, it's also important to validate your feelings, to allow yourself time to adjust to a new way of living and can even be a time of grief for some. The critical point is to not allow yourself to get stuck there and follow that path, otherwise ailments such as depression and/or anxiety can occur. To deny negative feelings is to push them to the side to breed and grow in the background. If we don't address how we feel, if we don't engage with others, then we are only setting ourselves up to fail to feel powerless and miserable again.

I realise it didn't help when we heard words like lockdown, isolation, limits, stopped, enforced, taken away and other similar words consistently. The repetition only reinforced the notion that we weren't in control of our lives and nothing could be done about it and to a certain extent, that was accurate. It is accepting that events such as these belong in our circle of concern – outside our influence and aren't worth wasting time focusing on what we were powerless to control. We couldn't control the pandemic, but we could control our response to it. Understanding this and implementing the gr rule, will help combat feelings of helplessness in future. Acknowledging it was hard, it was tough on all of us, is an important step for healing and moving forward. It builds strength and resilience as well. We need to be aware that these types of situations can be the catalyst for negativity and a crippling mindset, that can affect a person's self-worth if we choose to focus our attention this way in the future.

The recent pandemic saw an astronomical rise in people consuming alcohol at home and a rise in domestic violence as well. We saw lines of individuals waiting to buy copious amounts of alcohol to help them 'feel better'. Using alcohol as a crutch to numb their feelings in a blanket of intoxication is not sustaining, certainly unfulfilling long term and does nothing to solve the problem. It only compounds it.

Alcohol has been proven to have direct links to suicide, domestic violence, depression and anxiety and during situations such as these where we were forced into isolation, consuming alcohol does nothing to aid a positive mindset. How does alcohol help the situation during a global pandemic? It only aids in furthering potential ailments and fuelling dormant issues that can spur depression and anxiety symptoms on. Using alcohol as a means to cope is not one that's sustaining, it certainly won't help transform your life – it will only set you back. Alcohol does nothing but kill vital brain cells, inhibit development and is a great companion for negativity and a victim mentality.

Your mind can be your greatest weapon for you or against you, but how you choose to use it will then determine the experiences you have in the world. What we tell ourselves, what we choose to allow to reign in our minds, what we choose to focus on will grow in strength. Whether you choose to allow negativity to take over and sell yourself short is ultimately your decision to make. You can deny the fact that it is your responsibility to choose wisely in order to live a happy and productive life – that's up to you. But we need to take a closer look at the power of positivity and gratitude in living a better life, to help you understand that you are worth more than what you may be currently settling for.

If you deny the fact that you are worthy of more it's time to put away the excuses. It is time to grow up. You're an adult now, a mature and responsible person who is trying to better themselves and it starts right here. As I've said before, you may have had it tough, yes you may have missed out on opportunities or not had enough money to do the things you wanted to in life, but guess what? So have other people and they didn't use self-pity as a reason not to achieve. They didn't blame others for the way their lives turned out, they grew up and got on with it. They took responsibility, became exceedingly grateful and humble and realised that life was waiting for them right at their feet. All they had to do was pick it up with a truckload of self-belief, a little self-confidence and walk down the road of knowledge, to learn the skills they needed to live extraordinary lives. Not only that, they then were so empowered, so grateful for all the opportunities they encountered, that their willingness to help others became a priority. You cannot give of that which you don't have to give and it all starts with you.

Unless we face up to ourselves then nothing will change. Sometimes a bit of tough love is needed for individuals to be prompted to take action. As a coach, I see people with so much potential who aren't willing to do the work necessary to become extraordinary. At times I feel like saying, 'wake up to yourself, you're amazing'. I don't of course, as that would not be respecting where they're at. I have to be patient and guide those clients who are willing to walk the path of self-discovery, but in doing so, I give out a dish or two of tough love, because ultimately I care.

I can't tell you that you are worth it if you don't believe it yourself. What I can say is, start believing today that you are, start believing today you can do this. Start with grabbing a bit of gratitude and implementing the gr rule and do it consistently every day and watch how things start changing. Even if you don't feel you are at this moment, do it anyway.

How we language things will determine the experiences we have and what those experiences will be like. Becoming aware of what we say to not only ourselves but to others as well, is another important step we need to take to get the most out of life. Our words, our thoughts, our actions and our deeds, can empower us and propel us forward or the opposite is true. It's all about choice and being responsible. It's maturity in action, deciding that you are worth more than just settling. Unless we become aware of the language we choose to use and how powerful those words are, then we cannot change it.

In the words of Dr Phil, 'You cannot change what you don't acknowledge' and this applies to the choice of words we decide to use. It starts by implementing just a little more gratitude in our daily lives, practising the gr rule every moment we can, to change the experiences we want to have. We all want to live a happy and fulfilling life and how much joy, happiness and personal fulfilment we experience will be influenced by how much gratitude we give to one another and ourselves.

Some exercises for you to complete to help improve your gratitude and confidence levels to shift your thinking patterns to serve you better:

- What are you thankful for today?
- What do you spend your day doing? Write down the activities that are stimulating your mind and those that aren't. Start eliminating or minimising any activities that aren't enhancing your health and vitality.
- Buy a journal and for a minimum of thirty days write a reflection for each day that documents your growth. You only need ten minutes per day to do it, but it's important to record it as we tend to forget otherwise. You can focus on:
  1. What you're grateful/thankful for
  2. What specific actions you've taken that's helped create lasting change

How you decide to write in your journal is up to you. You can choose to write poetry, songs, essay format – the choice is yours. The important thing is that you commit to doing it at the end of each day, focusing on all that you're grateful for and all the positive aspects of your day – especially those we take for granted. It may sound a little simple, but trust me it works!

As with any new habit you're forming, it takes time to become an automated habit. Give yourself time to get used to doing this consistently and if you forget to do an entry, don't let that be a reason to slip back into the habit of beating yourself up again with negative self-talk. You're an adult now who has decided to take responsibility for your life and using the gr rule consistently starts with only ten minutes per day commitment.

You don't have to tell anyone about it, you don't need to be held publicly accountable for the change you're making, it's up to you at this point to prove to yourself you can do it. You can increase your gratitude, you can widen the light of positivity and it begins now.

Tool 12

Mind your language

"The more thankful I became, the more my bounty increased. That's because – for sure – what you focus on expands. When you focus on the goodness in life, you create more of it."

Oprah Winfrey

For many years I was very sick and underwent countless operations and spent months at a time in hospital. On occasions it was due to recovering from surgery and other times from complications caused by surgery. What I didn't realise at the time was that my mindset and what I talked about was adding fuel to the fire. It was crippling me mentally, reinforcing a negative mindset and slowing my recovery. This had a ripple effect too, whereby when I went home, the conversations I continued to have with loved ones, usually centred around my health and it was one of the reasons I ended up developing depression and anxiety.

The conversations I was having with doctors, nurses, family and friends were all centred around how bad things were, how tough I had it and how I was justified in feeling the way I did. What it was doing was reinforcing my negative thoughts, by talking about the negative aspects of my illness and recovery, as opposed to the positive ones. If there were positive elements spoken about, they were far outweighed by the negative ones. I felt comfortable, too comfortable, and felt I had every right to feel the way I did and these were the things that dominated my conversations with others. What didn't help, was that some others who were in my circle, also reinforced that feeling I had of being justified and that helped cushion the comfortability factor even more for me.

Admittedly, it was hard and that's worthy of recognition. Those years were really tough coping with being poked and prodded and operated on, leaving scars over my body and arms. What I didn't realise then was the power of the spoken word, the power behind what we speak and its effects on the type of experiences we have in life. I was inadvertently reinforcing my mindset by speaking about the negative aspects of my health to the exclusion of all else. My health became the dominant conversation starter with anyone I came in contact with, thereby eliminating the possibilities that go with positive thinking and its effects on living an extraordinary life. I had no clue. I was perpetually stuck with no idea how to help myself.

How we create our world can either empower or disempower us. The way I was languaging things back then disempowered me. Looking back though, I didn't have the luxury of education around a positive mindset, of being grateful to the extent I am now, or the power of the spoken word to change and influence how I experienced the world in which I lived. My reality back then was very dark, bleak and morbid. I had the victim mentality and I was comfortable not being challenged. I didn't have the necessary 'know-how' to change how things were and those around me didn't either. Life revolved around being sick, in hospital, in pain or under the surgeon's knife. I was happy letting others decide my fate, I didn't feel I had a voice to stand up for myself and take part in my own health care, because I lacked the confidence to do so. My mindset was one of allowing the professionals to make all the decisions for me. After all, they knew better *(said with a sarcastic tone)*. They were in control and I was just along for the ride, I didn't have the technical knowledge that they did, so I felt justified in sitting back and not taking responsibility for myself. I stayed silent.

Staying silent only went to reinforce my lack of ability to take responsibility for how I recovered in and out of hospital. Conversations with others that focused predominately on the negative aspects of my health issues, only helped to reinforce negative thoughts, negative feelings and a negative experience of the world resulted. I didn't know how to change things, I had no idea of how to help myself and felt completely powerless as a result.

Now, however, with all that I have experienced, with all the knowledge, study and clients I have coached, I am well and truly armed with empowerment, positivity and a belt of gratitude to hold it all. What I talk about now as opposed to what I spoke about then, are two entirely different worlds which create two very different realities. The blessings I see from all those hospitals stays, from all the darkness and pain I have encountered in life, is the ability to relate on a personal level with others. Having walked in their shoes, I can honestly say, I understand – I totally get it. Using all the darkness I've encountered to shine light on others is an incredible gift in itself.

Language plays a central role in defining and constructing meaning in the world. As my own experiences have shown, I had created a very different reality for myself in those years, as opposed to the type of life I am still experiencing today. It's the fuel to empower our desires and to direct and align positive energy. Commensurate to this is negative energy. The way in which we use words to construct our interactions with the world around us, can be greatly influenced by the type of environment we've been raised in. Culture, ethnicity and religious beliefs also play a part in the choice of words we use and have a high impact on our experiences as well. Our words have the power to decide whether the world in which we live, the reality we create for ourselves, is a positive and empowering one or a negative and disempowering one.

Studies have shown that a person's self-image is reflected in the words that they use. Negative thoughts narrow our mind and cut off other possibilities, thereby decreasing the amount of positive light that can be shone in our lives. Our focus becomes disproportionate, which can prevent us from noticing or recalling the positive aspects of a given moment.

Have you ever noticed that when you recall an event that wasn't entirely enjoyable, that all you seem to remember is how it negatively impacted you? That all you seem to remember are the bad times? This can be very real for some people and a great example is adults who grew up in domestically violent homes, that don't have particularly fond memories of their childhood. More than likely, they'll recall the events that impacted them in a negative way, as these were the experiences that left their mark. That's not to say this is a deliberate exclusion on their part, not at all. But their ability to recall happy moments from their childhood are scattered, disjointed and scarce and consequently, haven't impacted their memories to the same extent as the negative and painful ones.

Events such as these can have lifelong ramifications if the individual doesn't realise the power behind what they verbalise, because it can create a very negative and limiting reality in the years to come. If all they talk about is negative moments, if all they've predominantly experienced are painful and difficult events, then their ability to experience an abundance of positivity is extremely unlikely. These events do not define us – they don't have to impact our future selves, if we decide we are worthy of more than the limitations negativity causes.

Our past doesn't define our future, our experiences don't decide how we interact in the world – we do. How we language things now, how we interact in any given moment within our environment, within our circle of influence and particularly with our inner selves, determines and shapes the reality we experience. There is no one singular reality – there are only versions of it. How we decide to create that world of ours is entirely up to us.

Part of creating this is forgiving the pain and heartache from the past. Letting go of the events that caused terrible pain can be an arduous task for some, but it's a way to free ourselves from the chains of the past. At some point in time, we have to grow up and recognise that now as adults, we are in charge and it is time to take responsibility. Part of that responsibility is breaking old habits from the past and learning new and better ways of doing things, including changing our language patterns.

I'd like to add here, that it's easy to fall into the trap of 'I wish I'd known this stuff back then' type sentiments. Back then, we weren't in the position we are today, we didn't have the choices that we do now because we simply didn't know. Being kind to ourselves when these moments confront us is extremely important, because if we did know then what we know now, we would have done it. Beating ourselves up for past mistakes or experiences where we weren't armed with the knowledge we have now to help with those issues is a fruitless exercise.

How we decide to live our lives and choose to experience every moment is a decision that only you and I can make. We can't rely on anyone else to do for us. It takes maturity and a sense of worthiness to recognise the need to change what we say to ourselves and what we talk about with others. Words are powerful enough to hurt people and likewise, they're powerful enough to build them up as well. I'm sure you've heard the saying 'sticks and stones may break my bones, but names will never hurt me'. Whoever came up with this saying has obviously never been on the receiving end of name calling, because words *do* damage people. They may not in a physical sense, but they certainly do in an emotional, psychological, social or even spiritual one.

As I stated earlier, we are not defined by our past nor does it determine the type of future we design for ourselves. It's liberating knowing we have the choice in how we live and being happy and content is exactly that – a choice. Being sad and miserable is also a choice. The truth is, you can determine how much satisfaction, joy, tranquillity and happiness you want to experience in your life, by sharpening the tool of empowerment. We need to make a conscious effort to become aware of the language choices we make on a daily basis, if we are to help change our lives for the better and develop a greater sense of confidence and self-worth.

Language is a gift we've been given and it is a bit like breathing; it becomes automated. We don't think about breathing we just do it. The same can be said with the words we choose to use. The words we choose to use are predominantly influenced by the environment in which we were raised and is therefore limited. We are not exposed to a wider range of language choice until we are independent and mature and even then, we are limited by the conversation choices we have with others, particularly those we choose to be around. Unless we are exposed to a vast array of experiences with people who are different to ourselves, our language will be limited. That's why learning is such a critical tool in developing confidence and becoming empowered.

Because language can become automated, that we talk about things without really being too aware of the words we use (the exception is cussing of course), we can become oblivious to how our words affect us and others as well. Many of the words we use come with an emotional charge and can heighten the way we feel and react in different situations. When we use words stacked with negative emotions, we trigger a physiological flight or fight response. This response was designed naturally to help us flee from scary or threatening situations and not to manage the everyday trials and tribulations of the modern environment.

If you take the emotion of anger and if you say that out loud, it comes with an automatic charge like an electromagnet, that makes anyone else around you feel its intensity. For example, if I say, 'I am angry because the item I was expecting to be completed by a member of my team isn't done' it sends out a great deal of negativity and only serves to disempower those around me. It makes others feel worthless, unloved and far from being respected. However, if I said, 'I feel disappointed that the item I was expecting to be completed isn't done' instead, it has less impact on the other person and doesn't damage their confidence levels. The amount of emotional charge that being angry has, to that of being disappointed, is vastly different and carries less intensity.

When I first became aware of the power of the spoken word and how it can change our everyday lives, it was so enlightening. Knowing that I was in control of the type of experiences I wanted to have each day and not being answerable to anyone but myself, was quite a wakeup call and it felt truly freeing as well. I would often catch myself saying phrases like 'I don't

have to do... if I don't want to' or 'I can choose to do ... if I feel like it.'
Knowing that I had my power back, that I had the freedom to choose how
I experienced things, by the language I chose to use, was truly satisfying. It
felt almost like I had been let out of a cage. I felt happy and content again.
I felt free, powerful and strong.

It's an important aspect of developing true self-confidence and being
independent, realising that you are only answerable to yourself. As Leon
Brown stated, "No-one has power over you unless you give it to them,
you are in control of your life and your choices decide your own fate."
Having that realisation that no-one controlled me, no-one else could do
that unless I allowed them to, was in some aspects a little confronting and
at the same time truly exhilarating. We are not answerable for anything we
do in life with regard to self-development and our positive interactions
with others to anyone else except ourselves. Giving yourself time to adjust
to this new found freedom is very important, because being aware of the
power of language both to self and others, will be the catalyst you need to
project you forward in life. How you do that, whether in an empowering
or disempowering way is entirely your decision to make. Being mindful
of the language you use brings it into your conscious awareness and is
therefore, creating a new and improved habit to replace those old habits
that no longer serve you.

The following table is a great starting point to identify what type of phrases
and words are empowering or disempowering and how they can have a
dramatic influence on our thoughts, feelings and actions. The idea is to
use this as a guide to help you make better choices with the words you
choose to use to create the world you want to experience.

Disempowering Language	Empowering Language
I can't	I choose not to
Why me?	How can I?
What does it matter?	How can I show I care?

They are wrong	We have a difference of opinion
I hate	I prefer/I dislike
Destroyed	Setback
You make me feel	When you …I feel
You made me do	I chose to
You are wrong	Let's discuss it
I feel anxious	I'm bothered, unsure
I don't have a choice	There's always a choice
There isn't enough time	I prioritise what's important
I'm only	I am
I'm just	I am
That's bad	That's interesting, that's different
I should/ You should	I could/ You could
I have to	I choose to
I need to	It's important to me to
Always/ never	Seldom/ sometimes/ often
I can't	I'm not willing to do/ I am willing to do
I'm so overwhelmed	I'm a bit busy, I'm challenged
I'm angry	I'm annoyed/ frustrated
It's too hard	It's challenging
I'll try	I'll do it/ I'll do my best
I'm okay	I feel fabulous/ I'm wonderful
I should	I could
I should've / could've	Next time I will
I'm hopeless	I'm hopeful
I'm such a failure	I made an error in judgement

I didn't have a choice	I always have a choice
Everything is going wrong	I'm experiencing a setback
It's shocking/ terrible/ disastrous	Things could always be worse
I must do	I'd like to
I might	I will
I don't know	I don't know yet
My weakness is	I have room to grow/ improve

Through my reflections, I have discovered that six key factors influence whether or not empowering language becomes a regular habit. These factors are commitment, choice, maturity, responsibility, action and power. I'll explain each of these key factors a little further, but the table gives you a great reference point to begin changing your language and identifying some of the phrases you use. Anytime you're unsure whether the language you are using is helping you or not, you can refer to the table above and then apply the six key factors in your own life.

The first of these is commitment. If we want to change our language from disempowering to empowering, we need to commit to the process of changing it. Holding yourself accountable to your actions, becoming aware of the language choices you make, will help shape your daily life. Commitment to yourself, commitment to the process of change enables growth and understanding and with growth and understanding, comes empowerment and transformation. Without committing to the process of change, then things will remain exactly as they are.

The second factor is choice. We all have choices in everything we do in life and the same applies to the type of language we use. For example, I choose not to swear, I choose not to include it in my vocabulary at all. Even when I hurt myself or something traumatic happens I do not swear. I've chosen to exclude it entirely from my vocabulary. This has been a process too and it was by applying the first key factor of commitment, that I became more aware of my language choices and in the pursuit of bettering myself,

I chose to use other adjectives to describe the situation or event that was happening.

As a result of this, my language became more empowering and positive, because even though the situation or event may have caused a knee jerk reaction to using expletives, I chose to find other words to describe how I felt. Classically I still use words like, 'wow', 'geez', 'jeepers', 'crumbs' and 'shivers' as the reactive language choice, but it was a conscious decision I made to improve my vocabulary to reflect my inner self. I find it offensive to use foul language or to be around others who use it and so I made the commitment to choose other words, because those particular type of words do not reflect the type of person I am.

By doing so, it improved my confidence levels and enabled my vocabulary to be improved as well. It doesn't diminish the intensity of what happened, it still gives it that emotional avoirdupois it warrants, given it is traumatic or a shock to the system. By choosing words that are not explicit or offensive, I found the payoff benefit was an improvement in self-worth too. It takes maturity to realise that these types of language choices do nothing to improve our self-worth, let alone our confidence levels.

I'm sure you or someone you know has experienced those awful stares or frowned looks from people when you've dropped an 'f' bomb in front of them and it's not a nice feeling knowing that what you just did impacted others negatively, leaving you rather red-faced and embarrassed. Swearing is disempowering and learning alternate ways to communicate what we are feeling, to explore the power of words and find other 'heavyweights' instead, gives you the same level of satisfaction in articulating what just happened, but without egg all over your face. You do have a choice and you do need to show some maturity in deciding that you are worth more than the 'f' bomb you chose to drop.

With choice comes responsibility and it goes hand in hand with maturity. Between stimulus (or the event), lies choice and making a responsible, empowering choice enables growth. How you choose to react to given events is a reflection of the type of person you are. Do you see yourself as weak and worthless or do you see yourself as strong, independent and lively? I hope that if you don't already feel the latter, you're well and truly on your way to doing so.

To enact positive choices, you have to choose to act in a way that helps empower you and not disempowers you. To create new and lasting habits, acting in a way that empowers you by consciously deciding to use different vocabulary, allows the transformational process to begin. Nothing changes without action and *not* acting is action as well; just not in a positive way. If you don't commit to the process and put these changes into action, then you'll remain stagnant.

The final factor or principle that influences these changes is power. You have the power to choose and what you do choose, will have powerful ramifications. You can choose to continue maintaining the status quo, without 'bucking the system', you can choose to continue to disempower yourself and reinforce the victim mentality or feeling powerless, or you can choose to do the opposite. Whichever way you decide to go each has payoffs or benefits. If you use disempowering words, then the payoff or benefit is that the growth of negativity and powerlessness will grow and intensify. However, if you decide to action empowering words consistently for at least one month, you'll have begun the process of enacting lasting, positive change. The power lies with you and only you can decide you're worth the effort to enact lasting change in your vocabulary usage.

It's worth noting that you need to practice being kind to yourself and not setting expectations too high initially to change your vocabulary choices. For example, if a person is using profanity interwoven in their everyday language regularly, then excluding all offensive language completely straight away would be setting the bar of expectation too high. This is setting ourselves up to fail and not to succeed and can also be a reason or justification, that we 'tried to change but it just didn't work'. We need to be mindful of the pitfalls we can encounter on our journey of transformation, that we don't fall into old habits again, feeling victimised, helpless and hopeless because we initially set the bar far too high. Once again we feel trapped by our own set of circumstances, making it seem okay that we stay the same because 'at least we tried'!

Committing to the process of change is imperative if lasting change is to occur. Keeping a journal helps track your progress by focusing on the areas in which you've improved, how your day has begun to change, how using different terminology is influencing how you perceive yourself and the world in which you interact. You can write some of the problems you may encounter, however, the idea is to have a concrete record of your progress so you can see how far you've come. It's easy to forget, but by reflecting and re-reading the pages you've journaled, you'll see how much positive change you've implemented.

Many health professionals suggest journaling to their clients about their anxiety and/or depression issues, focusing primarily on the negative impacts each of these respective illnesses has on a person. I'm certainly not suggesting that there isn't a place for this – that's not my area of expertise. What I am saying, is if we are at a stage in our lives whereby we are ready to take that step forward to creating a happier and joy-filled life, then focusing on the negative aspects in this particular instance is not recommended. In coaching, we help clients move forward that are ready for change, to transform their lives, but don't yet have the necessary knowledge or skill base to do so. Therefore, focusing on progress, on how things are moving forward in a positive way is of lasting benefit and highly recommended to do.

Using some of the examples of disempowering and empowering language phrases I listed, it will give you a better understanding of the power of language in creating an empowered or disempowered world. Add to that the intensity of negative emotions a person can feel and the power of the spoken word comes to life. Whereas, when we use positive and empowering terminology with positive emotions, a person feels uplifted, happy and centred. Words *do* have power and learning to use them to help make our emotions subservient and subdued and create a world in which the power of negativity is diminished, is the ultimate in self-transformation.

If we take the phrase 'I'm so overwhelmed' and think about its impact on ourselves, it creates a sense of helplessness and hopelessness, if it is part of our regular vocabulary. It has a finite tone of totality, like there aren't any other possible options or solutions and that there is no way out. It also carries a dark and heavy image like a heavy weight and it opens the door to negativity. As one client of mine put it, "It feels like I'm trudging through thick fog and mud and can't see my way forward." When this kind of thing happens, when we allow ourselves to feel overwhelmed and it costs our mental wellbeing, we end up with sporadic results or no results at all. This then reinforces the feeling of guilt for not achieving given tasks, validates the feelings of hopelessness and so the cycle continues.

I'm not sure if you've seen the movie Star Wars or not, but one of the main characters in the film Yoda, corrects Luke Skywalker's language when he says, "I'll try." As Yoda put it, "There is no try only do." There is no action in trying and no commitment. It is a nothing statement that doesn't give a conclusive indication of what a person will or won't do. It's wishy-washy at best and is in itself disempowering. Whereas, when Yoda corrects his language, it becomes active, committed and empowering as a result. It denotes choice, responsibility and maturity and Luke Skywalker then commits to the process of becoming a Jedi. Part of this process was a result of being corrected for using non-committal language. It now holds him accountable for his actions.

Classically, clients who continued to use 'I'll try' when supposedly committing to the process of change, told me without verbalising it, that they really couldn't be bothered. It told me everything. That one statement, coupled with other factors including their body language and the way they spoke, indicated quite clearly that they were not committed to the process of change. They were quite comfortable where they were. They were only interested in getting more attention and more reinforcement for 'how tough things were for them' and not committed to changing their lives. They were only interested in talking about the problem and not about solutions. Words have incredible power and a phrase like, 'I'll try' instead of 'I will' says a lot. It's a nothing statement that only adds fog and mud and not clarity and lightness.

I've encountered many women who have reached a stage in their life where they're not sure what to do with themselves. Their children have grown up, they're no longer working in a job that gives them immense satisfaction or others are simply seeking clarity for their future selves. These clients have hit a crossroad in their lives and some have felt disempowered, which is partly due to the type of language they were using. They didn't realise that the world they had created for themselves, the reality they were currently in, had its infancy with the words they were using. It did have a dramatic impact on how they felt, it heavily influenced their interactions with others and many were left feeling disillusioned and powerless. They felt like they had no choice in life, that they were answerable to everyone else but themselves and now when they were experiencing so much change in their circumstances, they didn't know what to do.

Case study: Anne

Anne is forty-eight years old with two grown children who moved out of the home and is a single parent. She was recently divorced and was left feeling isolated and alone and in her words, "I feel powerless, hopeless and worthless." As a result of Anne using these terms, she felt as if she didn't have any choice or control in how she was feeling and was therefore experiencing life in a depressed and miserable state.

It took Anne many sessions to understand the power in what she was saying and how this was impacting her daily life. She was unaware that what she was saying was in actuality, disempowering her and leaving her feeling empty and unfulfilled. She was experiencing life negatively and sadly and by focusing her attention on the words she chose to use, slowly but surely Anne began to experience a whole new reality, one in which she felt greater sustainability and self-confidence.

Anne's story isn't unique in the sense that many of us have been left feeling a similar way after a divorce or major life-changing event, but learning new and improved ways to interact with others helps us gain mastery and control of our lives again. It's at these crossroads when we can get truly excited, instead of the complete opposite. Changing how we language things impacts our map of the world, how we perceive things become positive and nothing that happens to us or around us, has a lasting negative impact. We've decided to take the journey of empowerment and empower ourselves through positive language choices.

As I mentioned earlier in the book, the Covid19 experience left many people feeling disempowered, but others have seen it as an opportunity to do things they normally wouldn't have the time to do. This incident has been a major life event, leaving some people traumatised, powerless, victimised and negative. Their view of the world has only grown in a negative way, because they've chosen to focus on the negative aspects of it and not seen it as an opportunity to do other things. In part it may be due to a lack of knowledge and understanding and partly due to the high levels of negative language being pilfered into their consciousness. I wouldn't have had time to write this book if the whole Covid19 thing hadn't happened. It has been an opportunity for me personally to grow, reflect, write and to rest. None of that would have been possible if it hadn't happened.

How we choose to view things and how we decide to interact with the world around us, takes maturity, understanding, getting educated about things that affect us personally and choosing to be empowered. Language carries an enormous amount of responsibility and is a major influencer in how we experience life. Empowering and disempowering language is a key factor in determining the type of experiences we have consistently. Each has payoffs and each impact our feelings and emotions. Disempowering language leaves us with little or no choice. It's bleak, dark, definitive and foggy and leaves a person feeling powerless and victimised and impacts a person's emotions negatively. It amplifies negativity and diminishes a person's ability to interact in the world in a positive way.

Unfortunately, one of the side effects of creating this type of experience for ourselves, is the possibility of anxiety and/or depression becoming part of our lives. Negativity has the power to affect a person's mental capacity, as well as manifesting itself in physiological symptoms. I'm not saying that a person who uses disempowering language, consciously or not, is the sole cause of a person being affected by these disorders – not at all. I do know, however, from experience and through coaching clients, that words do have an incredible ability to impact us. What we aren't often aware of is that we do have a choice, that we can turn things around for ourselves, we can create a happier and healthier reality, if we decide we are worth committing to the process of creating a better future for ourselves.

Committing to the process of empowering oneself through positive, empowering language takes time and practice. In NLP (neuro-linguistic program), we are taught about associations and how what we say impacts us in other ways too. For example, I mentioned earlier about a client I had who felt like she was in a fog and it felt confusing, dark and heavy. Those associated feelings she was experiencing were the NLP factors at work. Positive language choices can make us feel free like we are in control of the situation, that we're in the driver's seat and not in the passenger's seat, watching life go by without having a say in the direction it takes us. It is possible to be the navigator and the driver at the same time.

I often get asked, but where do I start? My answer to that is, just start. There is no beginning point that is right or wrong, it starts when you begin taking action to turn things around. A great starting point is to use the table I wrote earlier to help you, along with the key factors that influence empowering language as well. It's entirely up to you – but just start now. When we begin empowering ourselves with positive and optimistic language, the way we view things changes as a natural spin-off. As I've indicated, it gives us a sense of ownership and has the power to create new and exciting associations, which are lighter and widen the gap of choice. Empowering language assumes a person is mature, capable and responsible enough to decide that they are worthy of more than telling themselves how worthless they are.

It does mean a person is also accountable for the decisions and actions that they take. It naturally assumes we have goals, timetables mapped out and we keep appointments we've made. It gives us a sense of power, because we can have clarity and make purposeful decisions that propel us forward and not hold us back. We take ownership of our actions, we step up to the plate and we start the process of self-development with one hundred percent commitment and no excuses.

Excuses only give us a reason *not* to achieve and that is not the way we want to continue going. Excuses only justify why we don't achieve something giving us a reason to fail and failure is not an option anymore. If we take that journey again down the road of 'well I gave it a try and it didn't work out', that language articulates justifications, a lack of commitment and gives us a reason why failure becomes an option again. We've been down that road already and it didn't work out, so now it's time to action positive language instead.

Empowering language has a lighter feeling around it and denotes choice. It is colourful, articulate and powerful enough to transform lives. Instead of trudging through the mud with a foggy outlook, we can choose to alter our reality, by deciding to change the way we do things. By deciding to focus on the most important tasks to be done, putting a plan in place to achieve identified goals, it allows us to then shift our attention from feeling like we've achieved very little to nothing, to one of having a clear path forward and actionable.

Naturally, the language choices we make become different. We get excited by the prospects of completing tasks and not feeling powerless and confused anymore. Our language becomes brighter, has options and gives a sense of control, putting us back in the driver's seat once more. It takes practice and consistent effort to become good at driving and navigating. It takes practice and consistent effort to become good at enacting empowering language. You *can* do it, you can empower yourself and turn things around – you can transform your life. Remember to do nothing is action too; making an empowering decision today that has action and accountability in it will help you move forward in life. Breaking the cycle starts right now.

A suggested activity for you to do is as follows. You can put all of these things into your journal so you can keep track of your progress. Remember, there is no right or wrong when you do the suggested activities I've included in the book, they're designed to help you be brutally honest with yourself to help you learn and grow.

Questions for you:

1. What language do you use when you feel disempowered as opposed to empowered?

2. In what ways can you improve the language you are currently using in order to improve the quality of life you want to experience?

Tool 13

Voices matter

> *"Maturity doesn't mean age. It means sensitivity, manners and how you react."*
>
> Author unknown

There's a tonne of literature been written on the topic of effective communication and for that reason I've decided not to include a specific chapter on it. Having said that, there are a few key points that are worth noting about effective communication that will help empower you and improve your ability to communicate with others.

The best communicators are those who know themselves well and are able to articulate the spoken word in a mature, empathetic and intelligent way. They have the ability to put themselves in the shoes of the receiver and consistently check their level of understanding to avoid misunderstandings occurring. They speak with a smile in their voice and have a genuine interest in what's being said. They're aware and intuitive and always seek a win-win outcome for all parties concerned.

Besides turning our language choices around to become more empowering, we need to be mindful of *how* we say things too. How we say things can determine how it is received and interpreted and is a major factor in improving the quality of the way we communicate. How we say things matters and is highly influenced by our body language as well.

Growing up I would sometimes hear things like, stop whinging, don't do that and other types of phrases, that could be interpreted and viewed as being offensive, insulting or bossy even. But how those words are said including the tone, pitch, the volume they're said with and how a person holds themselves when saying them, will in part determine their impact on the receiver. That's why on social media when all we have to go on is the written word, we have to be mindful of not jumping to the wrong conclusion and pre-empting the intention behind it, because we don't have those other factors in play to help us understand properly. This is where misunderstandings can happen because people are quick to jump to the wrong conclusion. People's feelings often get hurt and relationships can be damaged if we don't look further than the spoken word.

I don't intend to go into great lengths about body language either as I believe this topic is pretty well understood by most. It does consist of around seventy to eighty percent of our language and influences how the spoken word is conveyed and perceived. Body language plays a huge part in how messages are received and interpreted and the spoken word itself makes up only around seven percent of impact alone. That's why how we say things matters and part of that are the tones or types of voices we use. These can be dived into three main categories: the adult (authoritative), the parent (authoritarian) and the child (permissive).

To some degree we all have these voices within us but to what extent we use them is different for every person. They're influenced by the environment in which we've been raised, by parents, teachers and the working environment. Part of developing our ideal voice is interwoven with maturity and being self-aware. Learning what voices are most effective in helping us in life is a pursuit worth taking. These voices we use a lot in our self-talk and in our interactions with others, and becoming aware and understanding the three main areas, we can then learn to adjust the volume switch on the ones that aren't that helpful.

The best voice to use is the adult voice as this works in perfect alignment with empowering language. It's mature, precise, offers alternatives and possible solutions and it doesn't judge. The other two voices – the parent and the child are different. To understand each a little more, I'll give you examples and some further insights so you can begin to recognise just which of the three you predominantly use right now, and if you need to adjust the dial and turn down any of the switches or if you need to turn one up.

The first of these is the parent voice. As the name suggests it is usually associated with our parents and/or our teachers and is the *taught* concept of life. When we use the parent voice it usually combines aggravated tones and aggressive style body language and can include gestures like finger-pointing, standing over people, looking down on others and can come across as being demanding. The type of language the parent voice uses is judgemental by nature and is very direct. When we use this tone regularly with others, it can be perceived as being bossy, over the top and tends to alienate work colleagues. When we use this voice on ourselves it can be to keep us in line. However, all that seems to do is reinforce the idea that we need that, that we aren't good enough to do things on our own and therefore need that pulling into line approach. The parent voice is usually angry and the volume on this switch is usually turned up quite loud. We need to be mindful of using this type of voice on others because let's face it, none of like being told what to do and none of us appreciates being bossed around by others. Especially when it is delivered angrily or aggressively.

Some examples of phrases of the parent voice are:

- "Don't do that, I told you already."
- "Do as I say."
- "You're so stupid, you should know."
- "You're useless."
- "If only you were more like…"
- "That's not the right way to do…"
- "You can't do anything right."
- "If you weren't so…then this wouldn't happen."

- "I've told you a million times already."
- "Are you thick or something?"
- "Do it this way."
- "You should do that."

There are many other examples, but the above phrases give you an understanding of the type of language the parent voice uses and how demeaning to a person these types of phrases are. They do nothing to help a person, nothing to enhance a person's confidence levels and nothing to help educate a person to become independent and think for themselves. It takes away the opportunity for sincere interaction, to create beneficial options and has a win-lose mentality. It doesn't see the conversation as equal; it doesn't create a sense of ease and purposefulness, and one person feels powerful and in control, (the one barking orders), whilst the other one feels demised and put down. That is the classic win-lose scenario and is one we don't want to emulate. The parent voice is the voice that pulls us into line without thinking through what impact the words have on the other person and is accompanied with aggressive and impatient body language and gestures. It's one voice we want to turn the volume down on.

We've all experienced the parent voice and we've all probably blurted out words and phrases similar to the ones I mentioned at some point in our lives. But when we do, we need to make every endeavour to pull back and sincerely apologise. I honestly believe there is no real worth in the parent voice with perhaps one or two exceptions.

If I was walking along the footpath with my young daughter and she suddenly ran towards the road, then yes, I'd pull her into line using the parent voice. I would yell, I would be quite over the top in the way I spoke and I'd be animated in the way I communicated because it's life and death – it warrants a shock to the system. At that moment, I need to get her attention and get it *now* because her safety is at risk. In this instance, using this type of voice to communicate is appropriate. But in my normal interactions with people, there's no need to use this particular type of voice.

On the flip side of this is the child's voice. It's the voice of our 'internal child' and is the one generally used to express how we feel when we are at either end of the emotional spectrum – angry or afraid. It is expressed from the experiences we have via seeing, hearing or feeling and is usually one we resort to when we aren't sure how to express our emotions maturely or we're having a temper tantrum and want our own way.

The child's voice can be seen as being needy and clingy and also the one we associate with being whinging and whining. When we use this type of voice as adults it can be quite unpleasant to be around. It's not an attractive style to use and people who use this particular type of voice regularly, tend to be defensive and exaggerated, and because they need to feel like they're in control and don't feel like they're being heard, they'll resort to this style. The phrases the child's voice use tend to be quite emotional and victimised and the accompanying body language are the shrugging of the shoulders, rolling eyes, stamping the feet, the dropped bottom lip and a vocalised whiny voice.

These type of people tend to be low in self-confidence and offset their need to feel complete by seeking a partner who is more authoritarian in style. Some like to be told what to do whilst others hate it. Either way, they avoid responsibility for themselves and constantly seek positive affirmations to feel good. Thus it becomes draining and tiresome to be around. They like to get their own way in whatever they choose to do and are the masters at emotional blackmailing. It can be manipulative and is destructive to relationships.

Some typical phrases include:

- "If you loved me you would…"
- "I hate it when you do…"
- "It's not fair."
- "What about me?"
- "It's their fault, not mine."
- "Things never go right for me."

- "I don't care."
- "You made me do it."
- "Don't blame me."
- "It's your fault."
- "This is the worst day of my life."

Words do have power and how we phrase things is a reflection of our level of self-worth and our confidence levels. If you've ever been around someone or used some of the phrases yourself, you'll notice how it impacted on the relationship in a negative way. When we use either the parent or child voice regularly, we are constantly looking outward for reassurance and affirmations – that we are 'all that' and it isn't healthy. People who constantly seek attention outwardly, whether using a parent or child voice, need to look within to see how they can further improve their self-worth. Those who aren't willing to improve themselves will see their relationships end in heartache and they definitely won't be sustainable long term.

If you look at some of the examples I gave above in both the parent and the child's voice, you'll notice a pattern in the language choice. Both types of voices are disempowering to either the giver or the receiver and more often than not they are to both. How we language things, how we conduct ourselves outwardly, is a great indicator of exactly how a person feels about themselves internally. When we choose to use either of these styles, we are eliminating choices, avoiding responsibility and the scenarios that play out are always either win-lose or lose-win. It will always cost someone something.

Both can be domineering and powerful and are at the expense of another human being. This is not what we want for ourselves or anyone else for that matter, so the ideal voice we aim for in life is the adult voice. The reason is that the authoritative style empowers us and denotes options and choice and a win-win approach. It indicates maturity, whit, empathy and envelopes responsibility. It does not cost anyone we interact with and this is ideal.

The adult voice is the voice of reason. It is value-driven, respectful and genuinely interested in what others have to say. When we use the adult voice when dealing with people who use the parent voice (who can be quite rude and aggressive), it allows us to stand our ground without bringing ourselves down to that level of conversation. It's able to reason when the other can't or won't, it is calm and concise and it never gets drawn into the emotional outbursts of others. It can deflect any potential harm that the parent or child voice may impart. The adult voice uses a firm and fair approach to conversations and always seeks to create a level playing field.

The authoritative style is the one used to discover how other people think and feel and is the ideal voice to resolve conflicts. If you're able to cast your mind back to a favourite teacher you had at school, they would have used the adult voice in their dealings with you and showed a genuine interest in your development. It's caring, compassionate and keeps an open mind. It's not judgemental and the voice is always calm. People who use this style can keep their emotions subdued and subservient to their intellect. They don't allow their emotions to take over, but can clearly articulate what they want to say regardless of the circumstances.

A point worth noting here, don't confuse calmness with being soft. Many people believe that to be assertive it means not being direct. Quite the opposite is true in fact. Those who are able to use the adult voice consistently are able to switch up the way they speak. They can be direct. They can be gentle. They use the other elements of communication to their advantage and they always come out on top.

Likewise, the body language that goes with it is attentive, leaning forward, smiling and engaging and is never threatening or is threatened. The type of phrases used tend to be respectful, comparative, informative and reasoned. Some typical phrases the adult voice may use include:

- "When you…I feel…"
- "What are our options in this situation?"
- "We agree to disagree."

- "How can this be resolved?"
- "I would like to recommend…"
- "I think, I feel, I realise, in my opinion…"
- "How would you like to proceed?"
- "You have a choice in the matter."
- "If you choose that behaviour, this is the likely outcome, or if you choose this one…"
- "What do you think, feel?"

The above phrases are only a sample of the type used in the adult approach, but it is always consultative, always provides options and it is always genuinely interested in having others involved where appropriate. When we implement the adult voice we find that our interactions with others improve and our circle of influence grows. It needs to also include non-threatening language, a firm and fair approach and consistency is the key. The adult voice has integrity, is value-driven, has purpose and meaning and is responsible by nature. Those who use it don't seek outside attention from other people for validation to make themselves feel better. They seek to validate instead. Using this type of voice consistently will empower us and not only that, will help to empower others.

Questions for you:

1. What voice do you find yourself typically using in your interactions with others? How does that differ from the voice you use with your self-talk?

2. How do you respond to others when they choose to use the parent or child voice?

3. What improvements can you make today that will help develop the authoritative voice and implement it consistently? Try making a list of typical phrases you use and re-word them where necessary. Note the changes you make in your journal.

Tool 14

Are you listening to me?

"Most people do not listen with the intent to understand; they listen with the intent to reply."

Stephen R. Covey

A key part of effective communication and self-improvement is listening. How many of us have used the phrase, 'are you listening to me'? Particularly when we talk with our children or significant other. I know I have. Typically, the response is either 'yeah, I am' or 'uh-huh' which indicates they aren't tuned in and paying attention, but tuned out and not interested. They may hear the words being said, they may even be able to relay back what we said. The lesson for us is, we need to start tuning in and giving our full attention, instead of tuning out and only hearing the words.

This begs the question, how does this help empower us? The fact is, unless we are giving people the time, space and a genuine presence, then it reflects poorly on us. If we aren't giving someone our full attention, wanting to understand them and what they have to say, then it is a great indication of the level of worth we place not only on them, but on ourselves as well. It comes down to respect and respecting the person, space and process and respecting ourselves enough to put others' needs before our own. We need to learn how to be fully present during those conversations.

We've all experienced a time when someone looked disinterested in what's being said and appeared to be totally self-absorbed. They're holding their mobile phone, scrolling through Facebook, rather than giving us their full attention and giving the occasional grunt in response to what's being said. It's one of those classic situations when we would ask, are you listening to me?

Unfortunately, when we aren't self-confident, when we are a little unsure of ourselves, it can manifest itself in anti-social behaviour – one of which is being an ineffective listener. Ineffective listening is in my opinion anti-social. As I said earlier, if we aren't respecting the space enough to give our full attention to others, then that's an issue. It is anti-social. When a person doesn't feel good about themselves they tune out and escape to 'the world according to Facebook' as a means of comfort and feeling in control of their life. This is just an example of course, but I'm sure you understand my point. When we haven't had the opportunity to develop the skills to become an effective listener – an empathetic listener, then the reactive behaviour can be to disengage completely. It's a safety mechanism so a person doesn't look silly or feel embarrassed, because the truth is they haven't yet developed the skills to tune in. Otherwise they would.

A person has to have a willingness to learn how to listen with the intent to understand what others are saying, otherwise it's pointless. It's normal to want to be heard first and have others listen, but an empathic listener takes it to the next level. They're aware of all the cues, using their senses to gauge the space they're engaging in. They take notice of not only the spoken word, but the non-verbal cues such as body language and take a genuine interest in what others have to say. Even when a person doesn't feel like talking or engaging, we need to seek to understand where they're coming from first, before pushing what we want to say onto them.

We need to be mindful of the space we use when we engage in conversations with others and remind ourselves to be genuinely interested in what they have to say. We want to understand them and we reflect this in the way we engage with them. The issue for some, however, is that although effective listening skills are a major part of communication, we just haven't been taught *how* to listen properly. It has been assumed we all know how to. When you consider the fact that listening is an integral part of communication, it begs the question why aren't we all taught this skill? We are taught how to read, how to write and how to speak, but very few of us, if any, are taught the skills needed to be an empathic listener.

With that in mind, I believe that a lot of misunderstandings and hurt feelings could be avoided if we learned this skill. We are often so quick to fix the problem before us, that we don't take the time to listen effectively and can misinterpret what the issue is really about. We come with preconceived ideas and notions about what we *think* the problem is and offer quick-fire solutions. When we take this approach, we aren't validating the person's feelings nor are we being congruent with our own values. Taking the time to understand how a person feels and what's on their mind, allows *us* to be validated as well. When we help other people it makes us feel good. So listening properly has its benefits for us as well.

Consider the following scenario:

"Mum, can I talk to you about something?"

"Yeah sure, what's on your mind?"

"You're going to think it's really silly and stupid though."

"No I won't, tell me."

"You promise you won't get mad?"

"Yes I promise, now what is it?!" (said impatiently)

"I don't want to go to school anymore, I hate it."

"What do you mean you don't want to go to school anymore? After everything I've done for you, you're telling me this?! You can't throw away your education, just because you don't feel like going, it doesn't work that way. When I was your age..."

As the example indicates, Mum isn't listening intending to understand what's really going on. She is quick to jump in and remind her child about the importance of an education and how much she sacrificed to give her that. The problem is she hasn't really listened to what her child is feeling and has therefore, not resolved the underlining issue at all. She hasn't read between the lines and has missed the opportunity to be genuinely present. What's she's inadvertently done, is made it all about herself by focusing on the words she's hearing, excluded all other cues and has not addressed the underlying issue. Her inability to put herself in her child's shoes (to be empathetic), has eluded her and has damaged not only the conversation, but potentially the relationship as well. The problem remains a problem.

Sadly, it's an example I see all too often. When we bring our own experiences into the conversation and are preparing an answer in response to what's being said, then we aren't listening as we ought to be. On top of that, the classic line, 'when I was your age…' just doesn't work. It reflects you aren't interested in what's being said, but rather only interested in sharing your own story and giving your opinion. You expect people to listen with the intention of understanding you and what you have to say, yet the same expectations aren't being fulfilled when the roles are reversed. If we are to develop true authenticity, true transformation and self-confidence to the best of our abilities, then we need to make sure that our outward behaviours are aligned with our core values. Part of this is being an empathetic listener, who takes a genuine interest in others and what others have to say as well as what they feel.

Consider the same scenario, but now with the intent to understand:

"Mum, can I talk to you about something?"

"Yeah sure, what's on your mind?"

"You're going to think it's really silly and stupid though."

"No I won't, tell me."

"You promise you won't get mad?"

"Yes, I promise, what is it sweetheart, what's the matter?" (said with empathy)

"I don't want to go to school anymore, I hate it."

"Why do you feel like that? Tell me more about it."

This scenario indicates not only an intention to understand the situation better, but also has a change in what's said and *how* it's said. This conversation shows compassion, a genuine desire to understand the other's point of view and it is all done with a great deal of patience. The space, the child and the Mum are all being validated and respected as opposed to scenario one. You'll also notice that the last sentence is completely different and being an open-ended question, it has now opened up the conversation and allowed both of them room for exploration. It suspends judgement as well.

I can picture the Mum and child sitting down together using direct eye contact, warm and engaging tones and relaxed body language gestures. The tone used would be calm and soothing and the volume turned down low. The conversation has a new air about it. It shows true empathy and compassion. Mum is demonstrating she is genuinely interested in not only validating her child's feelings, but to resolving the underlying issue as well. This space has ensured her child feels safe and secure to open up without the fear of judgement or rejection. It is ideal.

When we are interacting with loved ones, we need to be sure we are seen as being authentic and aligned with our core values. If we behave in an abrupt, unapproachable and inpatient way, the likelihood of others coming to us when they are in genuine need is minimal. The same goes for our children. We need to create a safe space that doesn't judge and allows them the freedom to be vulnerable. Children can only emulate what they see and learn in their environments and to avoid making mistakes like scenario one, we need to be sure we are providing an environment that is conducive to open communication now and for the future. If we aren't demonstrating and living it, how on earth can they?

Children having an amazing ability to see duplicity, to see what's real and what's not and if they sense in any way that you're not being true to character, then they won't trust you. If you're the kind of person who is loving, funny, open and caring, then they'll instinctively trust you (unless proven otherwise). If, however, you behave one way in private and another in public, this automatically sets off alarm bells and they'll resort to protecting themselves and distrust you.

When adults, who as children, have been exposed to environments where they were rejected or made to feel inferior, tend to grow up with low self-esteem which affects how confident they are. Their ability to trust others is deeply affected and it takes much longer to gain their trust. This is completely understandable and therefore, we need to be mindful of *who* we open up to. If we open up and talk about our feelings to the wrong person it can be soul-destroying. If that person breaks our trust, it can be a catalyst for beating ourselves up for trusting too soon. Avoid that trap. Take it as a lesson and move on. Wolves can wear sheep's clothing and it is important to acknowledge that you haven't always got a radar to instinctively know whether you can trust someone completely or not.

As adults we need to remember that we need to see congruency in behaviours from people. We need to see others living out their core values and being open, kind, honest individuals who deeply care and listen to others. Trust is earned by observation and engagement. It is earned by communicating – by talking and especially by listening. It is listening with the intent to understand and reserving judgement and providing a safe place for others to do so. It's where we need to be.

The fact of the matter is we can't trust everyone. We should be able to but we can't. We are all born instinctively to trust, help, love and nurture one another, but somewhere along the way some people who experienced difficult situations, learned to put their guard up as a means of protecting themselves. When we learn to trust again, to bring down those walls, it's a reflection of the level of trust we have learned to have with ourselves. When our confidence is at an all-time high, we know that even when others let us down, even when they do break our trust, it won't affect us personally and our core selves remain strong and firm. We won't allow them to take our personal power away and do that to us. Our confidence isn't affected because we have learned that trusting ourselves and our abilities, are superior to and not dependent upon, the level of trust we have in others.

Remember that like attracts like; therefore, it is a natural phenomenon that those who have high confidence levels will naturally attract others who do too and their capacity and ability to trust is a reflection of the same. Creating an environment that is safe, loving and secure is the ultimate level we want to achieve. Becoming an empathic listener is the highest level of the five levels of listening skills.

The five levels of listening skills are as follows:

1. Ignoring – The lowest level of listening is called ignoring – not listening at all. People at this level consistently are preoccupied with themselves or other things and are not paying attention to what's being spoken about and can be physically disengaged as well. Their body language will be directed away from the speaker showing a total disregard for the conversation. Their body language will be closed down with signs like crossed arms, slumped shoulders, turned away and little to no eye contact at all.

2. Pretend listening – Pretend listening is most easily explained in the face-to-face conversations with others, where the other person has that blank look on their face and seems to be 'off with the pixies'. Responses at this level tend to be phrases like, 'Yep', 'Okay', 'Uh-huh' and are repeated intermittently throughout the conversation. Often the person speaking will be clued into the recipient not listening properly and classically may ask them, are you listening to me? Did

you hear what I said? Typically, the response will come back, 'Uh-huh' or 'Yep!' When this happens you know they're not listening and the conversation is futile.

3. Selective listening – During selective listening we pay attention to the speaker as long as they are talking about things we like or agree with. However, if they move onto a topic that we have no interest in or care about, we tend to slip back into either the pretend or ignore mode of listening. Growing up, I heard my parents talk about my grandfather as having selective hearing and it always made me laugh. He would do exactly that; tune into what he liked to discuss and tune out when subjects came up that he had no interest in at all. He could get away with it though, because he was older. The older generation have got permission to tune out!

4. Attentive listening – Attentive listening occurs when we listen to the other person, but while they are speaking we are deciding whether we agree or disagree and determining whether we think they are right or wrong. Instead of paying close attention to the person, we are formulating our response to what he or she is saying. People in the attentive listening phase may use terms like, 'I know exactly how you feel' or 'I know what you mean'. Further to this, they then proceed to interject into the conversation and tell you all about their own experience before giving the courtesy to just listen – and listen attentively. When we are at this level, we are already preparing our responses in our minds to where we believe the conversation is heading and interjecting with our judgements and opinions based on our own maps, beliefs and values. We are wearing our own set of glasses and prescribing the view in which the speaker *should* be seeing things. At all four levels, it should be evident that we are listening to our perspective and in most cases, with the intent to respond from our own experiences and map of the world.

5. The fifth and final level of listening is known as empathic listening and this is at the top of the listening skills ladder. This is where we should aim

to be. It is the highest form of listening skills and allows a person to put themselves in the shoes of another person and listen with the intention of understanding. An example of this is in the area of customer support. We've all experienced both good and bad customer service, but it's the ability of the service operator to understand their customers' needs, that will make one company stand out from another. It takes time, patience and understanding to be an empathic listener, but the benefits for both make this level of listening a win-win scenario as well. The customer walks away feeling as though they've been heard, guaranteeing them a positive experience and undoubtedly tells others about their experience as well. The customer service operator has successfully navigated through the issues the customer may have faced and had therefore, ensured return business. A win-win solution for both parties.

To achieve empathic listening, slow down, be patient, talk less and listen more and repeat back what was said to ensure you didn't miss anything and understand what they are trying to convey. An example phrase may be, 'What I'm hearing is…' (including the main part of what was conveyed to you), followed by, 'Have I understood you correctly?' Secondly, a question that encourages them to open up and tell you how it is affecting them shows true empathy. For example, 'How do you feel about that? I can only imagine how you're feeling right now.' This is just an example, but the idea is to validate their feelings, to convey to them that they matter and most importantly, that it matters to you that any issues get resolved.

A way to do this is to recap what was discussed, what approach you are suggesting to solve the problem and any follow up on yours or the user's part that may be required to solve it. It's important to be specific with *how* you will follow up. It may be by text message, email or a phone call. The important thing is that it suits you both and both are agreeable on the best way forward. It's also critical particularly in customer service-oriented careers, any tasks that needed addressing during the conversation that weren't resolved, are followed up and timestamped.

A great way to evaluate whether you're empathically listening or not is to ask yourself, where is my focus? This question allows you to check-in with yourself to see if you're seeing things from their point of view or your own. As you consider the first four levels of listening, think about the fact that the first four levels are self-focused, while the fifth level – empathic listening is focused entirely on them. When your focus is completely on the speaker and not on yourself, your level of service will be much higher and you will have achieved the highest and most useful level of listening skills in any situation you encounter. On top of that, you'll build better relationships both at work and home and gain the respect of people around you, by becoming a better listener. People notice these things and will learn to trust you on a much deeper level and will understand that you're a person who they can share their innermost thoughts and feelings with, without the fear of judgement or rejection. It's called integrity.

When we communicate with others, we are in actuality reflecting ourselves and our level of self-worth. If a person is constantly communicating negative, harsh comments and having frivolous conversations, it is a telling sign that there's something deeply wrong with them and *not* with you. We see the world through our own lenses, which is a reflection of how we feel about ourselves and not through anyone else's. We can at times assume that when we engage with people who have a toxic outlook and are on the receiving end of negative behaviour, that the problem must be us. Nothing could be further from the truth. The sad fact is, those individuals who are abusive, suffer tremendously from low self-esteem and have a poor identity with very little confidence. Yes, there are other issues undoubtedly tangled up with the issue, however, the point is, it is never *your* fault. When we learn the tools to transform our lives and implement them, we develop the confidence to deal with any situations we may encounter. We develop strength, wisdom, guidance and a deeper level of understanding and become people others strive to be like. We become tomorrow's leaders.

Question. What type of listener am I and how can I improve the quality of my listening skills?

Tool 15

⌀

Comparisons, comparisons

"The reason why we struggle with insecurity is because we compare our behind the scenes with everyone else's highlight reel."

Steven Furtick

Wanting to become a better person by improving ourselves is a walk we will undoubtedly take for the rest of our lives. It keeps us in check and allows us to stay humble and not to be in danger of becoming arrogant, as we know there will always be room to improve and grow. We will also have the attitude of wanting others to discover the joy and relief (in a sense), we feel as a result of developing confidence, whilst maintaining that humble and giving attitude.

Whilst we take this journey, it is a natural part of the human instinct to look to others to compare and decide for ourselves whether they are worthy to be emulated or not. In today's world, the screens are full of many role models both good and bad, but the danger is, some of us don't know which are suitable ones to be like and which aren't.

Whilst it is natural to make comparisons, the only real comparison to be made and the only one worthy of making is with ourselves. Taking this journey, celebrating change, embracing it wholeheartedly, allows us to see the positive growth that has taken place within ourselves. When we look back over that trek, we want to see that when we hit those rocky parts and came up against those pitfalls, we were able to overcome them with sheer grit and determination and we want to do all of that with our heads held high. Comparing ourselves to others is a standard we can't compare to, as we cannot make a true judgement on someone else's life with only some of the information. We don't know what people are like behind closed doors, so the only true comparison to make is with ourselves.

Having said that, there are many positive role models out there making a difference in the world and people like Oprah Winfrey and Tony Robbins immediately spring to mind. They've shared their trials and tribulations, been open and honest with their audience in the hope that their stories would be relatable. It gave people hope. These two amazing individuals have made it both in a financial sense and a personal sense. Again though, if I use myself as the example, the only true comparison I could make to them is not one I could make at all. How would I possibly measure that? How would I assess whether my growth is any better or worse than theirs? And if by doing so, I fell short of what I envisage their standards to be, how would that make me feel? Miserable, a failure, hopeless and all of those negative feelings and emotions could possibly be cemented within me. Yes, I can look at them and think they are amazing, they are doing a wonderful job in their chosen fields, but I cannot afford to let myself be so taken in by them, that their lives become the standard I measure my own by. This is a pointless and dangerous exercise to undertake.

I had this discussion recently with my neighbour and a few friends about making comparisons and we all agreed that it seemed a pointless exercise and yet we continue to do it. Why is that? Is there any benefit in making comparisons with others? If there are, what are they?

These questions were the fuel that set me on a course to research further to understand why people do compare and more importantly, was there a difference in the reasons why they were making comparisons? Did that have an impact on a person's view of themselves that was positive or was it negative and detrimental?

We all compare ourselves to other people whether we are aware of it or not, it's a natural part of the human psyche to do so. We do it even when the comparisons aren't meaningful, which is paradoxical to building self-confidence. Why would we continue to compare when all it seems to do is reinforce the self-belief we may have about ourselves that is negative? Curious and strange I know. Even when they make us unhappy, even when they don't make us better, smarter or more productive human beings, we continue this pattern of behaviour.

This is not a new phenomenon of the twenty-first century, human beings have always done it, but it's a topic that was never really discussed in days gone by. Personal growth and development has become the new 'in thing' and is a critical part of our growth and evolution that it does seem like a new thing. One reason for this is that it has come to the forefront of discussions on social media and articles centred around building confidence. But why do we compare and who do we compare to? How do we ensure that the people we are making comparisons to are ones that will help build our confidence in a healthy and enhancing way and not in a destructive and unhealthy way?

I know as a teenager I was compared with my brother throughout my schooling years by a teacher we both had in Woodwork. This teacher had taught my brother four years earlier than me, as there is a four-and-a-half-year age difference between my brother and I. Now my brother was not one of those teenagers who was confident enough to speak up and ask for help whenever he needed it and at times he would play up to the displeasure of Mr Smith, because he wasn't sure what to do sometimes. He was too afraid to ask for help. Mr Smith had made up his mind that my brother was one of the bad kids who didn't pay attention and therefore, warranted being targeted. My brother would often share how he was yelled at for not having the edge of the wood perfectly straight and smooth or the nails weren't fluxed with the woodgrain and how much that displeased Mr Smith. He would get yelled at and called hopeless or stupid and was unnecessarily and undeservingly labelled as 'one of those bad kids that just won't listen and behave'.

By the time I entered his classroom four years later, I too experienced this bias from him and the comparisons he made to my brother only stopped when my Mum confronted him about it during a parent/teacher interview. I was labelled automatically as being 'just like him' because we shared the same surname. This comparison, needless to say, had detrimental effects on both of us and caused unnecessary pain until my Mum came to the rescue. She was not one to take sides, but in this case after listening carefully to what both of us had to say, she ended the comparisons that night.

People constantly evaluate themselves and others in areas such as intelligence, attractiveness, wealth and success. According to some studies as much as ten percent of our thoughts involve comparisons of some kind. Social comparison theory is the idea that individuals determine their own social and personal worth based on how they stack up against others. The theory was developed in 1954 by psychologist Leon Festinger. Later research has shown that people who regularly compare themselves to others, may find the motivation to improve, but may also experience feelings of deep dissatisfaction, guilt or remorse and feelings of hopelessness and helplessness. When individuals start behaving in a way that reflects these feelings, they can end up with anti-social behavioural issues and even develop serious illnesses such as eating disorders.

But still, the question remains why is it we engage in this curious behaviour if it damages our self-esteem and feelings of self-worth? Why do we do it? Is there any benefit in engaging in comparisons to a person's wellbeing?

Human beings were designed with a desire to better themselves, to learn, to grow and evolve. It's only natural, therefore, to compare our standards with those we admire or are trying to emulate, because it gives us a reference point of comparison. Sometimes these can be unrealistic and disheartening, because the people we choose to compare ourselves to based on looks, wealth or intelligence, are often the ones that dawn the cover of Vogue magazine or the guy with the six-pack abs in the Nike advertisement.

In an attempt to want to better ourselves, what ends up happening, is that people realise that they can't stack up against them and then decide that it's pointless to improve and give up trying. They give up the effort required to lose the few pounds they'd set out to achieve, because the comparisons they've made are based on the polished Nike ad. When people feel the odds are impossible and stacked against them, that only goes to reinforce the negative mindset, which affects what actions, if any, they take. Comparisons are likelier to make us feel bad, when we make the error of only comparing ourselves to aspects of other people's best version of themselves. It can paint a very distorted picture indeed. Not that we realise that at the time, but that can have a negative impact on us.

People generally engage in either upward or downward comparisons. In upward comparisons, we compare ourselves with those we believe are better than us in some way and in downward comparisons we do the opposite. Research finds that downward comparisons makes us feel better about ourselves, but there are dangers to each approach; insecurity and jealousy or overconfidence and arrogance can result.

When we are comparing ourselves in a downward comparison, it is at the expense of others and can give us the feeling of superiority and can come across as being full of our own self-importance. Downwards comparison in the workplace, for example, may look something like the manager seeing himself as superior in what he or she does, that the type of work they engage in is better than the janitor's role of cleaning the toilets and bathrooms. This type of mindset, the 'better than thou' approach, only reinforces arrogance and self-confidence based on external measures. Therefore, it is precarious and dependent upon what others think of them. The person who engages in this type of comparison regularly, will never be internally satisfied nor self-confident in the long term. They are dependent upon external measurements to make them feel good, which will always be unstable and wavering.

As a way of compensating for their lack of self-worth, people who regularly engage in this type of behaviour can be aggressive in their approach and demeaning in the choice of words they use towards others, as this is a way of building themselves up to feel good. It's a power play. The win-lose mentality of these people means exactly that; they need to put others down to feel good about themselves and it is always at the expense of others feelings and emotions. These are not the type of people we need in our lives nor are they the type of people we want to emulate or compare ourselves to. These people regularly compare, they see life as one big competition in a dog eat dog world view and never feel truly satisfied or content with the way things are.

In upwards comparisons, we compare ourselves to those people we view as being better than ourselves and are using as role models to improve our lives. Again, caution needs to be exercised, as it can lead us down the path of self-destructive behaviour and negative self-talk, if we don't feel we live up to expected outcomes that we set for ourselves. We need to be sure that we aren't setting ourselves up to fail and therefore, have to be careful of who we choose to compare ourselves to. Are they worthy of being chosen? Are they the type of people we know well? If the goal is to be like them, why are we striving to be like them? Are we striving to be like them because they own nice clothes and drive a fast car or is it because they have a strong sense of self-worth and purpose in life and are exhibiting commitment in all they do?

If the answer to these questions is to improve our self-confidence by fine-tuning our values, beliefs, standards and expectations of ourselves that they emit, then that would be worthy of emulating. Do they hold themselves to high standards and have set and achieved goals in life? Are they a valued member of society, who always gives their best to do well in life and give back to others? Are they the kind of people who always seem to be popular with others because of their kindness and authenticity and not because they are demonstrative and overbearing? If the answer is the former, then they are worthy of our choice. All of these measurements are the internal, strong foundational core values, principles and qualities that we build upon to live purposeful and happy lives.

For example, my former hockey coach was one of those people who oozed a quiet confidence and was a fine example for me to follow. She was always team-oriented, inclusive by nature and lived congruently with her own set of values. Of course, she was fit and highly skilled, but what I admired the most about her and what I implemented in my own life, was her desire to help improve others' lives by being the example herself. It wasn't just about being a skilled hockey player or being match fit and ready, it was about so much more than that. It was that genuine care and compassion, that genuine interest in other people and what they had to say which affected me the most. All the qualities she naturally exhibited, had a flow-on effect to all areas of her life, including the hockey pitch. That gave her credibility, authenticity and was a fine example to follow.

These types of role models are the types we look to emulate. We don't spend hours a day daydreaming about them, but when we make comparisons like this in the hope of improving our own lives, we can look to them as a type of reference point of where we would like to be in life as well. We don't want to put them up on a peddle stool like an idol to be worshipped, but they're the type of people who make a lasting impact on us for all the right reasons. They don't dawn the cover of Vogue magazine or have the six-pack abs, but by comparing ourselves to people like my coach, it makes our desire for self-improvement a realistic and achievable goal. They are within our circle of influence and they are the people we strive to be like, but we don't make the comparisons based on superficial qualities or upon how much they own or have. Their standards and expectations they have of themselves are high and they live congruently with their core values and beliefs.

With that in mind, I didn't spend my time focusing on my coach to improve my own life, but her influence on me was such a positive one that it left its mark. To this day, I still use her as an example of the type of person who impacted my life in a positive way. These are the people who inspire others to better themselves and never judge a person's intellect, capabilities or any other aspect of their life. They push us to be better human beings and believe in us even when we may not believe in ourselves and their impact is life-changing.

Still the question remains, how can you make a fair comparison? If I was cooking a cake and scones for example, the recipes for both require different quantities to make them what they are. Each requires a baseline of measurement and if I wanted to improve the quality of my cakes and scones, how could I possibly compare the cake to the scone to measure whether they've improved or not? That would be a waste of time and a ridiculous notion to suggest to someone. They are two very different items each needing different ingredients, different quantities and cooking times. Therefore, comparing them to each other is a waste of time.

If I focused on wanting to improve the quality of my cakes, the only way I could measure whether or not my cakes had improved in taste, presentation and quality, are to compare it to the previous cakes I had cooked. It would also be based on the feedback I received from those consuming my product, to give me ways they could be improved. If I based my adjustments I made to the recipe, method of cooking or the way I presented my cakes based solely on the feedback of others, it wouldn't give me a fair assessment. The consumer wouldn't know the ingredient list or the method I used to prepare the cakes – only what they see and experience with the end product. The end product is polished and presented to look enticing for the consumer and the customer doesn't see the effort taken to get it to that stage.

Therefore, we need to be mindful that when we are wanting to improve ourselves, we don't make comparisons based solely on what we see (in part) or experience. It is much more than that. Just like cooking the cakes, it has a specific list of ingredients that make the cake the unique type it is. It has a specific way of preparing it; whipping the egg whites, folding through the sifted flour and the cooking time. Making the cakes as special as they are and as special as I envisage them to be, cannot be based solely on what others think of them. I need to take note of the ingredients, their brands, the measurements I use, the way I blend it, the way I cook it and for how long. It's only the final stage in the presentation for others to consume, do the opinions of others come into the mix. Therefore, making that comparison based only on part of the information to improve my cakes is a waste of time, because it is an unfair assessment to make.

However, if I had kept track of my progress from when I first started cooking and what ingredients I used, how I prepared and presented them, then I have a baseline for comparison. It's only by comparing the cake itself from where it was to where it is now and where I envisage the end product being, that a fair comparison can be made. If I had invested the time in noting down my progress to achieve my goal of having a quality, well presented and tasting cake, then that's worthy of my time. Investing time comparing my cake to others is just not worth it. If I consistently do this type of behaviour, I am in danger of becoming upset, disheartened and even jealous of the quality that others present.

The only benefit of comparison is for self-improvement. If I do compare my cake to someone else's who I believe has a better cake that I want to use for myself, then asking for the recipe, following a tried and tested method of cooking is a smart move. Why re-invent the wheel when the recipe for success is staring you in the face? I can decide to present it the way I want putting my individuality into its presentation, but the ingredients and the method are a proven system that works. This type of approach would be great for budding entrepreneurs or those looking to others for help in new areas of development. However, when we are on the path for developing confidence, for finding true meaning and purpose in life, we need to abandon comparative behaviour and adopt the mindset of self-improvement instead.

Comparisons are a waste of our time as we cannot compare our behind the scenes with everyone else's highlight reels if we want to experience true success in life. Achieving that internal peace is not achieved by looking outwards and comparing ourselves with others. It's an internal, progressive journey that can only be made by us and only compared with ourselves. Progressing our growth, keeping a journal and monitoring the ups and downs, allows us to celebrate how far we have come and achieved. It's easy to forget how brave and courageous we are, but when we look back on our journey by keeping a detailed journal, it can be an empowering and powerful read. It's also a great reminder how far we've come as we tend to forget the steps we've taken to improve.

We need to learn to be kinder to ourselves and not be the harsh critic who judges others highlight reels with our everyday moments. It's unrealistic and it's not the reality. The only comparison worthy of our time is our own. Remember, just like the cake is unique – so are we. We all have our individual gifts and talents, so isn't it time we celebrated those gifts and stopped making unrealistic comparisons? Of course, it is.

Questions for you:

1. What comparative behaviours do you engage in? Are they helpful? If not, what will you do about this?

2. What role models do you look to? Do you need to adjust who you aspire to be like?

3. Make a list of people you admire that are inspirational to you. How well do you know them? Are they worthy of being emulated? If so, why?

4. Commit today to stop unhealthy comparisons and make a commitment to yourself to track your progress. Remember the only comparison worthy of your time is to yourself.

Tool 16

It's not about time management

"It is not enough to be busy...The question is: What are we busy about?"

Henry David Thoreau

So far I've spoken about a lot of tools that will help you shift from a negative mindset, to one that is powerful, empowered and full of energy. Many of my clients have spoken to me about the issue of not being clear and knowing how to move forward with their life. Clearing the fog and seeing the light that shows us the way forward, will keep expanding through the implementation of these tools. The next tool I want to introduce is centred around how we use our time.

When clients are in that haze it can seem all-consuming. I hope that by trying out these tried and tested tools, you too will experience great personal and professional success like they have. Sometimes we need someone independent from ourselves to give us the guiding hand we need to navigate through these new learnings. By now you're aware that eliminating old habits without replacing them with new and improved ones doesn't work. We cannot simply take away old, repetitive forms of behaviour without replacing those with something else – it just won't be sustainable that way. Willpower will only get us so far and having a clear focus and knowing why it's so important to change, is a critical step for lasting self-improvement.

Without a one hundred percent commitment to yourself with action in your words nothing will change. The same old procrastinating habits will re-surface, the big to-do lists and goals will lay stagnant and unfulfilled. By now you know how to break the cycle of negative self-talk and you know it's by committing to purposeful action. Talking about it does nothing. Doing it does.

A great place to start is to look at where our time goes. Stephen Covey's *Seven Habits of Highly Effective People* (which I've referred to throughout the book), is where I first learned about the time management quadrant and its application for assessing how we use our time. It's a tool I've adapted and refined for my own clients to use, as a means of assessing how they use their time and if the activities they participate in produce real results. The more I have used the time management quadrant, the more ideas I've had around its usage and effectiveness, as a way of helping people adjust their habits to become more personally fulfilling and productive.

By using the time management quadrant, we have a visual representation of how we use our time and whether we need to adjust things or not. Sometimes it's not until we see where our time is going and how much time we are spending on different things we do each day, that we get a real indication of whether the activities we habitually do help us or not.

In the following time management quadrant, I have used a student as the example. Others I have seen from participants in my courses, have been very specific about what they included in the quadrant. Some chose to include time they spent thinking about things they'd like to achieve, some chose to even include cooking and grooming times. How you decide to use it is your choice, but to get really clear and see its effectiveness in your own life, you need to get specific with listing all the activities you do. Following on from this, I asked each participant to add up the total amount of time they spent in each quadrant, to get a fair assessment of whether their habits were helpful or impeding their progress forward.

The following is an adaptation of Covey's time management quadrant.

Time-Management Matrix (Example for a student)		
	Urgent	Not Urgent
Important	Quadrant 1 – Emergencies and Crises *Examples:* Death, illness, accidents. Writing an essay, the night before it's due.	Quadrant 2 – Takes Planning: you, relationships, school, work, maintenance of material things *Examples:* Filling in all test dates, assignment due dates, academic deadlines, breaks, holidays and special days on a semester planner. Joining a club for exercise. Studying on a regular basis.
Not Important	Quadrant 3 – Other People's Problems *Examples:* Going with a friend to see the tutor about their assignment because they feel nervous. Helping someone choose an outfit for graduation and driving them around town.	Quadrant 4 – Time Wasters *Examples:* Surfing the internet for travel deals when you don't have the time or money to travel. Scrolling mindlessly through Facebook. Reviewing course material that you are already knowledgeable about. Watching re-runs on television.

Time management has always been associated with being more organised, that if you weren't an organised and structured person, you didn't manage time very well. It isn't just a matter of being more organised or managing time better, it's about using that time more effectively to reap the results you seek. We all have the same amount of time to use, so when it comes to using our time more productively and effectively, we need to get honest with ourselves if we intend to change things for the better. Once that's understood, the application of the quadrant becomes a very useful tool to use, because you can see the purpose behind it in helping you to improve your quality of life and your identified life goals.

The term 'managing time better' denotes a certain level of intelligence, that if a person doesn't manage their time well, they are somehow seen as being ineffective. Instead of managing time better, it's about deciding what is important, what takes priority, in what sequence this occurs and for how long we do them for. Forming new and improved habits that help us use our time more wisely, takes practice and commitment and as a natural consequence of implementing, a person's level of confidence rises.

In quadrant one, the associated activities are pressing, urgent and important. They need to be addressed or done *now*. They can include things such as health emergencies for example, which if aren't addressed immediately could end in permanent injury, disability or even death. The interesting point to note is, that some health issues that end up in this quadrant, may have been avoided by being more proactive with the health issue at hand. If, for example, a person had a heart attack due to obesity, by being more active and health-conscious in quadrant two, the person may have avoided the emergency room visit. This is the point of quadrant two; to be proactive and plan, organise and implement activities that are important to everyday life, but don't have the urgency of quadrant one.

Quadrant one activities are time-sensitive. People who primarily identify with this category end up feeling stressed, frazzled and over-worked. Many CEO's enjoy working under such conditions, but they are also the ones with chronic health issues, tattered marriages, fractured relationships and burnout at a young age. When we operate from this category on a regular or permanent basis, these are the type of results we get. We may get the job done, but with better planning and organisation, (quadrant two), we could have avoided the negative consequences that resulted from being in this constant state of alertness.

People in quadrant one feel they are constantly under the pump and some fluctuate between this quadrant and quadrant four activities, procrastinating and wasting time for a variety of reasons. It may be they enjoy the pressure to get things done now or struggle with being more disciplined and organised or maybe it's simply a behaviour they are used to doing. Putting things off until the last minute and not prioritizing the things that are important to them, end up becoming urgent quadrant one activities. This causes them to fall into a predictable pattern of behaviour. They're either feeling pressured for time or wondering what to do with themselves, when they aren't in this constant state of stress and alertness. They lack balance.

For example, a student at university who has a major assignment due in two weeks and believes he has plenty of time to complete it, decides to go and have some pizza and watch a movie marathon instead. Leaving things until the last minute, pulling an all-nighter to complete the assignment, he feels a sense of disappointment because it was so rushed and knows he could have performed better, if he had used his time more wisely. He knows quadrant one and four well.

The resultant outcome on his self-esteem and confidence are evident. He feels he has let himself and his professor down and knows he could have performed better. The C grading on his paper doesn't reflect his true capabilities and therefore, reinforces a negative mindset, telling himself 'I can't believe I did it again, geez I'm pathetic'. The cycle of this type of behaviour and negative self-talk continues, because he hasn't learned how to use his time more effectively and is relying on ingrained patterns of habits and behaviours. He is doing what he knows.

Therefore, the best place for us to be spending most of our time is in quadrant two. In quadrant two, there is time to think, plan, create and organise. This is where proactivity occurs and activities that have meaning and purpose. Quadrant two activities reinforce a positive mindset, helps develop self-confidence and is designed to help people be organised, structure activities that are important to them and achieve their goals. If the university student I mentioned above had scheduled a certain amount of time devoted to getting his assignment written over the two weeks, not only would the assignment been better planned and presented, but his grading would have been higher, reinforcing a positive self-image and a can-do attitude. Adopting new and improved behaviours of being organised, prioritising what's important and setting aside time to achieve what's planned, reinforces these new patterns of behaviour and thus the cycle of positivity and success continues.

In quadrant three the activities are usually about someone else's nonsense that you allowed yourself to get pulled into. Quadrant three activities need to be done now, but they aren't important, because they don't necessarily help you. Quadrant three activities are draining, leaving people feeling tired, like they haven't achieved anything meaningful for the day. People who identify with activities they do regularly that fall into this category, exhibit classic people-pleasing behaviours, where the priority becomes everyone else's business and they're left feeling unfulfilled. When individuals regularly do this, it can leave them feeling victimised and complaining constantly about not having enough time to get things done for themselves, as they're always doing things for others instead.

People in this category also find themselves in quadrant one; running around doing things last minute that they just 'didn't get a chance to do' for themselves. They often exhibit little patience, are fast-paced, finding it difficult to switch off and relax and are always playing catch-up. As a result, a self-righteous attitude can occur, where they think they're so important to helping others, they believe they are irreplaceable. That without them, nothing would get done.

That self-righteous attitude can be unsuspecting and can creep up on people, without them even realising they are developing this mentality. Understanding the traps of this quadrant, by putting others ahead of ourselves and self-righteously sacrificing for them, is leading us towards a life that's less than fulfilled. Feelings of resentment can occur if we continue to exhibit these behaviours, which can damage relationships.

Resenting others for taking valuable time away from you and blaming them for not having the time to devote to the things that are important to you, is a typical behaviour of this quadrant. It's toxic and unhealthy. Operating out of quadrant three consistently is settling for a life that's less than fulfilling. It's at the expense of yourself.

Quadrant four is full of activities that don't get us very far. We all do them – watching television, being on the internet without purpose, sitting around and chatting, reading a magazine and so on. The unimportant and non-urgent activities are time wasters, unless you intentionally plan for them because they're important to you. If you plan for them because they're important to you, then they go into quadrant two. In that case, the activities have a place in your life and are called such things as relaxation, fun, entertainment or downtime. If you're watching television for five hours a night most nights, it's probably going to put most work that would ordinarily be in quadrant two into quadrant one – last-minute, high-pressured and high stakes. That's due to procrastinating and putting things off, putting unnecessary pressure on ourselves to get things done, that could easily have been avoided by prioritising them.

People who find themselves spending copious amounts of time in quadrant four, feel that life is just passing them by, that 'stuff just happens' to them, that they haven't got a choice in the matter and therefore find comfort in avoidance. These avoidance behaviours denote a lack of responsibility and maturity in decision making with few positive outcomes. People in this category feel unfulfilled, victimised and have low self-esteem. When we spend so much time wasting time, life just passes us by.

Case study one: Joanne

Joanne is married and a mother of two young children at primary school. Her husband works full time and with both children at school, she wasn't sure what to do with her time. She found herself feeling lost, reading magazines and watching the soapies on television and was consistently feeling tired and lonely. Joanne was always doing things for others as well and ended up feeling a little resentful, because those around her were happy and content and she wasn't. She felt she should be, being happily married for over ten years and two beautiful, healthy children, but she couldn't get past the feeling that something was missing.

Joanne came to me earlier this year complaining about being time poor and wanting to explore career options, but she had no idea what she wanted to do. Joanne described it well, saying she felt like she was in a fog and found herself consistently doing things for other people, leaving her no time to get things done for herself. She was great at making long to-do lists and setting unrealistic expectations around achieving dream goals and continually reinforced a negative self-belief that she was a failure, incompetent and hopeless, because she never got things done. This mindset of hers, then made it 'okay' for her to sit around and waste time. After all, what's the point in trying when they just don't get completed.

What we discovered during our sessions was that she was devoting hours each day to others' needs, unable to say no for fear of letting them down and was left feeling empty and confused. The amount of time she was devoting to quadrant three activities became apparent when she was given this exercise to complete.

For one week, Joanne was given the task of writing everything she did each day in her journal, so we could get an accurate assessment of where her time was going. Activities appeared in all four quadrants, but the amount of time devoted to quadrant three far outweighed the others. Joanne also found herself procrastinating a lot, engaging in mindless activities as a way of avoiding tasks she knew were important to get done. As a result, she found herself in quadrant one, finishing tasks at the last minute under the pressure of time.

Joanne exhibited classic people-pleasing behaviours, too afraid to say no in case she came across as being mean and heartless. This meant she was constantly sacrificing what was important to her to help everyone else get *their* tasks done. What she soon realised, was that she was not devoting time to what was important to *her*. Even though she wasn't too sure exactly what career she wanted, the fact was she was avoiding taking responsibility for herself to find out, by doing things for others instead. This justified her behaviours, justified not achieving her own goals and it justified her constantly complaining that she was time-poor. It hadn't occurred to her that her own actions were costing her the happiness and personal fulfilment she sought.

This case study highlights an important aspect that I see all too often; women feeling that they must sacrifice themselves and their happiness to make sure that everyone else is feeling happy and content. Yes, it is normal for women who are mothers to want to make sure their children are happy and moving ahead in life, but that doesn't mean it is at the expense of themselves either. It's not an either/or scenario, where if one is happy then the other can't be – it's the opposite. As mothers, we need to demonstrate through positive role modelling, how to get ahead in life, how we can choose to be happy regardless of circumstances and learn to use our time wisely, to ensure a positive and optimistic future. It's not our job or responsibility to sacrifice ourselves to please everyone else. That's not the kind of role models we want to be.

Case study two: Ian

Ian is a middle aged professional mechanic who recently went into business for himself. He is married with three adult children not living at home and employs a fulltime mechanic to work with him in the business. His wife has retired from the workforce and is keen to support her husband in his new venture. Recently, he decided to employ an apprentice and since transitioning into business ownership, Ian's time with his wife has suffered as a result of spending long hours catching up on paperwork for the business. Ian used to enjoy a spot of fishing with his mates once a month, but since owning the business, he hasn't been fishing with them. Ian enjoyed this get-together as it helped him relax and unwind and helped keep a close bond with his friends.

Ian's transition into business ownership had the intention of setting himself and his wife up financially, so they could enjoy their retirement together hassle-free. He loves his work and thrives on the challenge of finding what the problem is with the mechanics of different makes and models of cars and fixing them to full working order again. Sadly, his relationship with his wife, Marg, was starting to suffer because of the amount of time Ian spent developing his business model and making sure that things ran smoothly. He was trying to do it all – be the mechanic, bookkeeper, receptionist and office manager and train the apprentice. All of this whilst learning how to run his business effectively, so it would turn over a profit. Ian was coming home exhausted and irritable and started to feel a little resentful towards the business.

He didn't have other skills other than being a highly trained and skilful mechanic and felt he was out of his depth. He began to question his decision of going into business for himself, whether he had made the most colossal mistake of his life, by investing their retirement money into buying the business. Ian was an all-in all-out kind of guy, who often made decisions on a whim, without really doing all the necessary work to fully understand what's involved in new ventures. This was one of those decisions. Not that he regretted buying the business, but he did wonder if he had made the right decision without knowing all the ins and outs of the business world.

When Ian came to me for coaching, he had several issues to work through, but the main concern for Ian (so he thought), was not having enough time to do it all. Being new to owning a business, Ian needed to learn ways to delegate some of the responsibilities he was carrying himself to be more effective. The way things were going, Ian was headed for some major health issues, brought on by stress. He was missing the time he spent with his friends fishing and his marriage was in trouble too. Ian's issues ran much deeper than managing his time better, but on the surface it appeared he just didn't have enough hours in the day to do all the things he wanted to.

Together we formulated a plan that would help Ian better utilise his time in the area he was passionate about, which was being a mechanic and training his apprentice. The constant worry of having to do it all, was weighing heavily on his mind and he didn't want to see his business fail. He had invested all of their savings to fulfil his lifelong dream of owning a mechanic shop, but the daily tasks of running a business kept Ian's mind in a constant state of worry. He missed his time fishing and he really missed the happy times he had experienced with his wife and wanted that all back. He just didn't know how it was all going to happen.

We started with the issue around time, as that's what Ian thought was the main problem in not achieving the goals he had outlined. Like Joanne, Ian kept a detailed log of his activities for one week and then transferred this into the time management quadrant. Ian spent a lot of time in quadrant one, feeling time-pressured to complete tasks and everything he was doing seemed to be urgent and needed dealing with immediately. There was little time spaced across the other three categories and Ian needed to get more proactive and organise his time better, to be more efficient and effective. What the time management quadrant uncovered, however, was deep-seated issues he was hanging onto which centred around fear and control.

One question I asked Ian was, "If you didn't spend your time worrying about all the things that have to be done, what would you be doing?" He looked at me as if I spoke Chinese to him. He looked totally confused and shocked by the question.

"Well, I would be working on the cars and training up my apprentice. I'd also be off fishing with my mates and Marg and I could start spending quality time together again. But how can I do that, when there's so much to think about? I'm worried because I don't know what to do about it all."

Again I probed, "How has worrying about all these things helped you?"

He replied, "Well I guess it hasn't, has it."

Ian realised that he had been spending so much time worrying about the issues about running an effective business, rather than formulating a plan with ideas on how to solve them. He was caught in this vicious cycle of negativity and inefficiency, that he couldn't see a way out of it and felt defeated. Ian was like a person treading water; barely afloat and unsure how much longer he could last if things didn't change.

The time management quadrant helped Ian see exactly where his time was going. With the aim of getting more productive, Ian realised he needed to shift most of that time into quadrant two, where proactivity and efficiency occurs. This was challenging for him. He also had to learn to relinquish control of certain tasks he was doing and learn to delegate some of them to other parties. Together we formulated a list of those tasks he could outsource, freeing him up to do more mechanical work in the shop. This was a major strategy he began to use and instead of worrying, he was now using that time to solve problems he was facing.

As our sessions together progressed, Ian would share some of the identified areas that he had chosen to delegate to other parties. Slowly over time, he began implementing these changes and he started seeing the merits in it. He now had an accountant taking care of the business taxation and bookkeeping requirements, his wife Marg was working part-time at the shop as the receptionist and office administrator, which also allowed them to spend more time together and Ian was feeling better about things.

I also referred Ian to a business coach to help him get a system in place that he was comfortable with. By working with them, Ian established a system that was easy to run and maintain, that freed him up to work on customers' cars and train his apprentice. What started with a fairly bleak and stressful outlook, now began to transition into having a profitable business ensuring a bright and successful future. Not only that, Ian now had time to go fishing with his mates once a month, had rekindled the romance back into his marriage and the business was now in a position to carry them forward into the future, without that constant pressure of time. Ian now experiences little stress as a result of these changes and having worked through some deep-seated issues, Ian is now free of the grip of fear and the need for autonomous control.

What these case studies illustrate, is that by becoming more aware of how we use our time, analysing whether or not the activities we partake in benefit us or not, we can learn to become people who are proactive and time-wise, instead of reactive and time-poor. With awareness comes change and with change comes improvement. It's when we are prepared to be frank about situations, that we can see areas we do well and areas where we can adjust to become more beneficial. It's always helpful to involve an independent person such as a coach, to guide you through new territory, who will assist you, challenge you and support you. They're impartial and will call you out if you aren't committing to actionable change and implementing new and improved habits that will serve you for the future. At this stage, that's exactly what's needed.

The next stage in the process is to remove old habits that are highlighted as holding you back and replace these habits with new and improved ones. We can't simply take away activities from quadrant four for example, without replacing them. We need to be wise when assessing what it is we want to be doing instead, which takes time, preparation and patience. For example, it could be quite easy to swap watching copious amounts of time watching television to reading the latest gossip magazine, but for what purpose or benefit would that be? Changing one bad habit for another bad habit does nothing to serve and nurture us. All it does is keep us exactly where we are – trapped, helpless, victimised and life just rolling on by.

It's important to be mindful of the type of activities we want to consistently engage in that stimulate our brains, moves our hearts and make us want to get out of bed in the mornings. If they aren't doing that, then why do them?

Questions for you:

1. How are you using your time? Try recording your activities for a week and transfer those to the time management quadrant. Where can you improve?

2. What activities do you need to change and replace with new and improved quadrant two activities?

Tool 17

A vision for the future

"A good plan well executed beats a brilliant plan poorly executed every time."

Author Unknown

"Don't lower your expectations to meet your performance. Raise your level of performance to meet your expectations."

Ralph Marston

I recently had a client come to me with issues around procrastination and not achieving the things she set out to do each day. She lacked clarity in the direction she wanted her life to take in so many facets including – spirituality, health and wellbeing, family and social and finally her career choice. What seemed so overwhelming to her, was the fact that she is an extremely bright person, who found it difficult to understand why she was in this predicament and the fact that she had such high expectations of herself, left her feeling less than satisfied.

She had the to-do lists, she had the long term dream that seemed a million miles away and had absolutely no idea on the steps to take to start experiencing success. It seemed insurmountable to her, but by formulating a plan and taking her through the process slowly, her confidence began to rise. Her days had previously been spent being busy doing nothing of real significance to her. However, now with targeted and meaningful tasks that were aligned with her own set of values and beliefs and incorporated her purpose statement, the vision board she created was a visual reminder each day of what it was she sought to accomplish.

Seeking clarity on a vision for the future is not an uncommon issue. In fact, most people at some point in their lives, are faced with the same problem of not knowing what direction their life should or potentially could take. Gaining clarity on what's important, will help make time spent each day purposeful, meaningful and build a person's self-esteem and confidence levels. One way that I found particularly useful to help gain that clarity, is to create a vision board that defines the main areas in life that are important for long term success.

This task at first can seem rather daunting, but taking the time to plan the board and thinking about what's important in your life, will help you get the clarity you seek. The areas that my client divided her goals and dreams into are a great example that can be used as a guide when creating your own. That's not to say that they're the only areas that are worth using – there are many other areas you could use such as the dream holiday, more quality time with others and allocated self-care time. From there it's about formulating a plan that is time-stamped, making you accountable to achieve the goals you identify as important and the steps needed to achieve them. As Stephen Covey stated in his book, *The Seven Habits of Highly Effective People*, "Begin with the end in mind."

Understanding the why when it comes to doing vision boards is important, because if we don't know the value of them and how much they can assist us in seeking clarity and building our confidence, then there's no point in doing it. I believe this exercise has so many benefits and the bonus is it opens the door to creativity. It helps affirm what's most important in our lives. Seeing it visually represented, allows us to have a constant reminder of why we do the things we do daily and gives us the all-important reasons for getting out of bed in the mornings.

Some of the other benefits of this exercise include:

- Get used to implementing new and improved habits
- Each goal achieved is a step forward to future success
- Combats procrastination and negativity and feelings of helplessness and hopelessness
- Replaces bad habits with new and improved ones
- Others see you focused and decisive in your actions, which allows you to share some of your successes with them
- Develops the intrinsic value of self-improvement and positive actionable change as opposed to relying on external measures for building self-worth
- Leads to greater personal integrity and a greater sense of satisfaction in doing things that are worthy and honourable and not just time fillers

Vision boards can encapsulate the different aspects of our lives and this task isn't meant to be set in concrete with how you set it out. It is meant to be a visual reminder of what your new focus will be that gives you the ability to plan each day in a proactive and meaningful way. The appointments and tasks in the diary aren't just filling space, making it look like we are such busy and productive people anymore. Now they have real meaning and purpose.

This is one of those activities that will help kick start positive change towards what you want to do in life. By starting with the smallest and easiest identified goals, it not only builds confidence, but gives you that all-important starting point. Often knowing where to start is a step that trips a lot of people up, because they have so many things they want to accomplish, they get swallowed up by the enormity of it all and simply give up. Knowing where to begin – that vital piece of direction, then gives them a way forward to completing the task.

People who would identify themselves as being perfectionists would relate well to this – having long lists, huge expectations and massive dreams that seem so far off in the distance, that they're 'out there' somewhere. They find it particularly difficult to kick start into action because of this issue of having so much they want to achieve, so many goals in life, that they fear if they start in the wrong area, everything else will go wrong or be a mistake. As one client described it, 'It's like being in a dimly lit room that has so many doors to pick from, but not knowing which one to go through first.' They become sub-consciously frozen, fearful of choosing the wrong door, for fear of failing and causing a domino effect to the rest of the areas of their lives.

But because perfectionists like to achieve and achieve well, they will appear extremely busy running around seemingly getting worthy things done, but at the end of the day are left feeling less than satisfied with what they've accomplished. In the mind of a perfectionist, it's better to be busy doing something than nothing at all, because it still gives them a sense of achievement. They also want to know it all *now* and if they don't know it all now, they're afraid of trying through fear of making a colossal mistake. They need to know what's behind all the doors first before they act. If they don't, they decline to do anything, creating a fearful cycle of negative thinking and behaviours.

It's better, therefore, to not act and weigh up all the options first, *appear* to be taking positive actions and taking copious amounts of time to do so, all the while telling themselves they're still being productive. Even when all the information is in front of them, they still fear choosing the wrong door and therefore don't act. The issue comes down to being confident to have a go and break the cycle of fear they're trapped by.

To illustrate my point, I am going to use my client as an example. Although her name and the details of her case remain confidential, it's a great way for you to understand this concept on a deeper and more meaningful level. As I mentioned, Claudia (my client), had identified four key areas of her life that were important for her to implement both for the here and now and for long term success.

The stumbling block for her, like so many, was knowing where to start and what actions to take first. She was experiencing a significant change in circumstances, with her children going to school and was needlessly suffering from not knowing what to do with herself. This issue is a common one for many women in similar positions. Claudia found that her normally high standards of cleaning the home were slipping, spending time watching television until it was almost time to pick the children up from school. She was feeling miserable and frustrated about her situation, because she knew she could do more, yet had no idea how to turn things around.

Claudia hadn't worked for almost ten years and now with her confidence in ruins, was spiralling downwards with no idea how to help herself. She's an extremely capable and intelligent person, but she felt that her skills were so out of date and not relevant anymore, that she began wondering what was the point in trying. The turning point came one day when as she put it, 'I just couldn't take being this way anymore' and reached out for help.

Often it takes desperation for us to act, to want more for ourselves and Claudia knew she wanted way more than what she was settling for. It's easy to become complacent, it's easy to choose to sit in front of the television, but as Claudia had begun to experience all too well, it was not satisfying in the slightest. In fact, the longer she continued this behaviour, the more her entire world began to suffer as a result. Her home was beginning to show the signs that something was wrong by not being as clean as tidy as normal, she was quieter and wasn't engaging with the children after school and was beginning to feel that she was a lost cause. She was telling herself she couldn't achieve her dreams, filling her head with so much negativity, that the light of hope was beginning to fade. When we met I asked Claudia some questions that I felt are an absolute must to be asked of anyone who wants to change their lives and who knows they're capable of more.

I began by asking her, "Why is this important to you? What is it that you really want out of life?"

She sighed and replied, "I really want to do more with my life, I just don't know how to get that anymore. I've tried but I just don't know what I want to do either. It's all a big mess right now and I feel like I'm drowning. I need help."

Claudia looked so defeated as she sat there staring at the carpet. She was confused and appeared to have no clear sense of direction in her life. Her eyes began to well up with tears and I could sense the desperation, as her voice quivered when she spoke. Her body language was slumped and forward with a heaviness only darkness and pain could hold and she was beginning to lose hope. As I probed further during our first session together, I could hear that she really wanted more for herself. When she told me she was committed to the process, I knew then that positive change was possible. If a person is truly wanting more for their lives, they must without any shadow of a doubt *want* it. If they are seeking an easy solution, then lasting change won't happen. They need to be prepared to put some work into helping themselves. I had to be sure she wasn't just seeking sympathy for her situation and was really ready to take that next step.

Transformation doesn't happen by giving someone sympathy – that only reinforces where they're at. I didn't want to be responsible for disempowering her any further by sympathetic validation, but rather acknowledge where she was at. I needed to be sure Claudia was willing to put in the work and was one hundred percent committed to the process, to get the positive changes she sought for her life. After our initial consultation was over, it was evident that this was Claudia's time to shine. She could sense hope that she could live a different type of life than the one she was currently experiencing and settling for. It's was only by deciding to get help and putting herself first, that she began to see she was worth much more. Claudia needed to break her patterns of behaviour and she needed a way forward.

We started with the smallest and easily achievable goals first. In the health and wellbeing section of her vision board she'd created, she identified that healthy eating had become a problem because she was feeling tired and lethargic a lot. Although this can be in part due to a poor mentality, she was right in concluding that her diet could be improved. When we spoke about this further, I asked why it was so important to her right now and why she had put this forward as an issue to be changed. Claudia told me that she had become complacent with her eating habits and her energy levels during the day were very low and nothing of real value was getting done. Her why for wanting things to change, was she not only wanted to feel better within herself, but she wanted more energy to start being more productive and proactive with her days.

By tackling the smallest of the four main areas of her life that were important to change, Claudia began to get the clarity she was desperately seeking. By starting with the smallest goals, Claudia's confidence grew as she slowly began to see the results of implementing new and improved eating habits. Even though she wouldn't see the immediate benefits of her healthy eating plan, that it would take time before her energy levels improved, Claudia stuck with it by constantly reminding herself why she was forming new habits. She was beginning to see the merits of being able to delay the need for instant gratification as a sign of growth and maturity.

The problem with human beings is we have this desire to have things now and our issues sorted and fixed asap. It would have been quite easy for her to give up because she couldn't see the immediate results of these changes, but she didn't. Claudia was able to foresee, that if she was patient enough with the process and waited until her body had a chance to get used to this new eating plan, she would eventually have the goal she desired – more energy and more focus during the day. Remember, it takes time to form new habits and to become routine, which wouldn't have been possible if she hadn't persisted and delayed that need.

When we begin implementing positive changes, it is not only important to have your eyes fixed firmly on the prize, but also remind yourself why it's important to you. Willpower will only last so long before it fizzles out and that reason why you wanted to improve things, becomes critical to lasting successful change. When identified plans are in place consistently, it no longer becomes a conscious effort to implement changes. It becomes automated.

Once a goal becomes the new normal, that the changes you made are not a conscious effort anymore, that's when you know you're ready for a new challenge to begin. When you're comfortable with the new normal you've created, you know it's time to take on a new goal and push the comfort zone once again, to incorporate more learnings for self-improvement. Claudia knew she was ready for a new goal from her vision board, because now she was consistently eating healthy foods and was reaping the benefits.

Vision boards are a great way to capture what truly matters to you and from there it is a matter of prioritising what's important, to use your time as effectively as possible to achieve personal success. When you start with the smaller goals first, you're creating the necessary building blocks of self-confidence to achieve more and more success, until you feel you've truly mastered all that you've set out to achieve. Remember though, when it comes to building our confidence levels, there will always be room for improvement, always new learnings and always new levels of growth. It keeps us in check with ourselves, that we are remaining true to our innate quality of being humble. Arrogance is never a good look and those with confidence know there's always room to improve.

When we experience new growth by pushing our comfort zones, it's a must to understand that you'll undoubtedly experience some levels of pain. Claudia experienced an initial amount of pain when she was adjusting to new eating habits, making her feel a little queasy, but after being patient and allowing her body time to adjust, the benefits were evident. We have to push past the initial pain, that initial phase of resistance we feel, if we want to reap the benefits of positive change.

Having a vision for the future is just that; it's a starting point to help redirect your time and effort towards actions that will benefit you in the short term, as well as in the long term. Going through some pain to experience long-lasting success in life, builds leadership skills, allowing us to be more resilient in the face of opposition and to develop responsibility, maturity and wisdom. Taking a firm and fair approach in life, allows us to stand firm with our values and beliefs and it encompasses a win-win attitude where everyone is on the same playing field and no-one is judged. The only judgement made, is whether or not the people we choose to surround ourselves with are people of influence and challenge, or those who hold us back. The choice is yours who you choose to have in your life, but by now I hope that those negative influences have been removed from your life.

Having learned some of the tools used when coaching clients with issues around confidence, I hope that you are now willing to transform your life too. Like a caterpillar becomes a butterfly, going through the stages of self-transformation into something truly unique and beautiful, you too, can shine your own light in the world. Be kind to yourself and be patient. Anything worth doing well takes time, effort and consistency is the key. You can achieve personal and professional success, all you have to do is decide you are worth it and do it. I wish you every success on your personal journey to living an extraordinary life. Remember, it's all within you.

Acknowledgements

Whatever endeavour we do in life, there are always people who help us along the way. This book is no exception. There are a number of people I'd like to thank for the roles they played in getting my book into printed format.

Firstly, Melissa Gijsbers my book coach who encouraged me to start writing and helped with the process of getting published, thank you.

To Connor and Jordan, I say thank you for being my independent readers and giving me honest appraisal of its content. I valued your input a great deal.

Lizzy and Mandy for assisting with the diagrams in the document.

Jodi for assisting with proof reading part of the manuscript.

To Jen from Fuzzy Flamingo for working with me to get the design from concept to reality and designing an amazing cover. Without your assistance this book would not be available for the reader. You're amazing Jen, thanks so much.

I am also very grateful to the endorsees who were good enough to give up some of their time to write their reviews for my book.

A special thank you to Robert Thatcher. You allowed me to read the chapters as I wrote them to you, giving me honest feedback and assisting with grammar and the flow of aspects of the book. Your friendship means a great deal to me.

I'd also like to acknowledge the love and support I have had from my best friend Julie Kennedy. Not only did you help me with the final proof read when I needed it the most, but also the emotional support was invaluable. Thanks Jules.

Finally, to God Almighty for giving me knowledge and experience and so much more. I feel so fortunate and blessed to be living out my purpose in life and part of that was writing a book that will undoubtedly improve lives. For Him who has captured my heart, I say, thank you.

Reference list

Oxford Dictionary website – Beliefs definition

Collins Dictionary website – Values definition

"The Seven Habits of Highly Effective People" Stephen Covey, Simon & Shuster, 1989, Model

Examples of purpose statements – source: internet

Indeed.com and Forbes.com (plus other related sites)

"The Seven Habits of Highly Effective People" Stephen Covey, Simon & Shuster, 1989, pp. 106-107

"The Seven Habits of Highly Effective People" Stephen Covey, Simon & Shuster, 1989, Rolfe Kerr Mission Statement, pp 106-107

"Have You Discovered Its Real Beauty" Dr Naji Ibrahim Arfaj, 2007

"Getting Ahead" Philip E. DeVol, Revised Australian Edition, September 2018, Hawker Brownlow Education, pp.86-87

"High Performance Habits" Brendon Burchard, Hay House, 2017, p.91 (excerpt)

TV show "Married At First Sight" – season 2020, Channel 9

"Seven Scientifically Proven Benefits of Gratitude That Will Motivate You To Give Thanks Year-Round" – 7 benefits, article published on psychologytoday.com

"Getting Ahead" Philip E. DeVol, Revised Australian Edition, September 2018, Hawker Brownlow Education, p.88

"The Seven Habits of Highly Effective People" Stephen Covey, Simon & Shuster, 1989, p.151 Time management quadrant